Willhelm Shakespear

Julius Caesar

A tragedy as it is now acted at the Theatre Royal

Willhelm Shakespear

Julius Caesar
A tragedy as it is now acted at the Theatre Royal

ISBN/EAN: 9783744640206

Printed in Europe, USA, Canada, Australia, Japan

Cover: Foto ©ninafisch / pixelio.de

More available books at **www.hansebooks.com**

Julius Cæsar:

A
TRAGEDY.

As it is now ACTED

AT THE

Theatre Royal.

WRITTEN BY

WILLIAM SHAKESPEARE.

LONDON,

Printed by *H. H* Jun. for *Hen. Herringman,* and *R. Bentley* in
Ruſſel-ſtreet in *Covent-Garden,* and ſold by *Joſeph Knight* and
Francis Saunders at the *Blew-Anchor* in the Lower Walk of the
New-Exchange in the *Strand.*

Dramatis Personæ.

JUlius Cæsar	By	Mr. *Goodman.*
Octavius Cæsar		Mr. *Porter.*
Antony		Mr. *Kynnaston.*
Brutus		Mr. *Betterton.*
Cassius		Mr. *Smith.*
Caska		Mr *Griffin.*
Trebonius		Mr. *Saunders.*
Conspirators { Ligarius		Mr. *Bowman.*
Decius Brutus		Mr. *Williams.*
Metellus Cimber		Mr. *Montfort.*
Cinna		Mr. *Carlile.*
Artimedorus		Mr. *Percival.*
Messala		Mr. *Wiltshier.*
And }		And
Titinius		Mr. *Gillo.*
Cinna *the Poet*		Mr. *Jevon.*
Flavius		Mr. *Norris.*
		Mr. *Underhill.*
Plebians }		Mr. *Lee.*
		Mr. *Bright.*

Women.

Calphurnia	Md. *Slingsby.*
Portia	Mrs. *Cook.*

Guards and Attendants.

Scene *ROME.*

THE

THE

TRAGEDY,

OF

JULIUS CÆSAR.

Actus Primus. Scæna Prima.

Enter Flavius, Casha, and certain Commoners over the Stage.

Flavius.

Hence : home you idle Creatures, get you home :
Is this a Holiday ? What, know you not
(Being Mechanical) you ought not to walk
Upon a labouring day, without the sign
Of your Profession ? Speak, what Trade art thou ?

Fla. Why Sir a Carpenter.

Cas. Where is thy Leather Apron, and thy Rule ?
What dost thou with thy best Apparel on ?
You Sir, what Trade are you ?

Cobl. Truly Sir, in respect of a fine Workman, I am but as you
would say, a Cobler.

Cas. But what Trade art thou ? Answer me directly.

Cobl. A Trade Sir, that I hope I may use, with a safe Conscience,
which is indeed Sir, a Mender of bad soles.

Fla. What Trade thou knave ? Thou naughty knave, what Trade ?

A 2   *Cobl.* Nay,

Cob. Nay I befeech you Sir, be not out with me : yet if you be out Sir, I can mend you.

Cas. What mean'ft thou by that? Mend me, thou fawcy Fellow?

Cob. Why Sir, Cobble you.

Fla. Thou art a Cobler, art thou ?

Cob. Truly Sir, all that I live by is with the Awl : I meddle with no Tradefmans matters, nor Womens matters ; but withal I am indeed. Sir, a Surgeon to old Shooes : when they are in great danger, I recover them. As proper men as ever trod upon Neats-Leather, have gone upon my handy work.

Fla. But wherefore art not in thy Shop to day ?
Why do'ft thou lead thefe men about the Streets ?

Cob. Truly Sir, to wear out their Shooes, to get my felf into more Work. But indeed Sir, we make Holyday to fee *Cæfar*, and to rejoyce in his Triumph.

Cas. Wherefore rejoyce ?
What Conqueft brings he home ?
What Tributaries follow him to *Rome* ?
To grace in Captive bonds his Chariot Wheels ?
You Blocks, you Stones, yea worfe than fenfelefs things :
O you hard hearts ! you cruel men of *Rome*,
Knew you not *Pompey* many time and oft ?
Have you climb'd up to Walls and Battlements,
To Towers and Windows ? Yea, to Chimney tops,
Your Infants in your Arms, and there have fate
The live-long day, with patient expectation,
To fee great *Pompey* pafs the Streets of *Rome* :
And when you faw his Chariot but appear,
Have you not made an Univerfal fhout,
That *Tyber* trembled underneath her banks
To hear the replication of your founds,
Made in her Concave Shores ?
And do you now put on your beft attyre ?
And do you now cull out a Holyday ?
And do you now ftrew Flowers in his way ?
That comes in Triumph over *Pompey*'s blood ?
Be gone,
Run to your Houfes, fall upon your Knees,
Pray to the Gods to intermit the plague
That needs muft light on this Ingratitude.

Fla. Go, go : Good Countrymen, and for this fault
Affemble all the poor men of your fort :
Draw them to *Tyber* banks, and weep your Tears
Into the Chanrel, till the loweft ftream
Do kifs the moft exalted Shores of all.

Exeunt all the Commoners.

See

See where their baseft mettle be not mov'd.
They vanifh tongue-tyed in their guiltineſs:
Go you down that way towads the Capitol,
This way will I: Difrobe the Images,
If you do find them deck'd with Ceremonies.

Cas. May we do ſo?
You know it is the feaſt of *Lupercal.*

Fla. It is no matter, let no Images
Be hung with *Cæfars* Trophies: I'le about,
And drive away the Vulgar from the Streets;
So do you too, where you perceive them thick.
Theſe growing Feathers pluck't from *Cæfars* wing,
Will make him fly and ordinary pitch,
Who elſe would ſoar above the view of Men,
And keep us all in ſervile fearfulneſs.

Enter Cæfar, Antony *for the Courſe,* Calphurnia, Portia, Decius, Cicero, Brutus, Caſſius, Caska *a Soothfayer: after them* Murellus *and* Flavis.

Cæf. Calphurnia.
Cas. Peace ho, *Cæfar* ſpeaks.
Cæf. Calphurnia.
Calph. Here my Lord.
Cæf. Stand you directly in *Antony's* way,
When he doth run his Courſe. *Antony.*
Ant. Cæfar, my Lord.
Cæf. Forget not in your ſpeed *Antony,*
To touch *Calphurnia:* for our Elders ſay,
The barren touched in this holy Chace,
Shake of their ſterile curſe.
Ant. I ſhall remember,
When *Cæfar* ſays, Do this, it is perform'd.
Cæf. Set on and leave no Ceremony out.
Sooth. Cæfar.
Cæf. Ha! Who calls?
Cas. Bid every noiſe be ſtill: peace yet again.
Cæf. Who is in the Preſs, that calls on me?
I hear a Tongue ſhriller than all the Muſick
Cry, *Cæfar:* Speak, *Cæfar* is turn'd to hear.
Sooth. Beware the *Ides* of *March.*
Cæf. What Man is that?
Bru. A Soothfayer bids you beware the *Ides* of *March.*
Cæf. Set him before me, let me ſee his face.
Caſſi. Fellow, come from the throng, look upon *Cæfar.*
Cæf. What ſay'ſt thou to me now? Speak once again,
Sooth. Beware the *Ides* of *March.*

Cæf. He

Caf. He is a Dreamer, let us leave him: Pafs.

Sennet. Exeunt. Manet. Brut. & Caff.

Caffi. Will you go fee the order of the Courfe?

Bru. Not I.

Caffi. I pray you do.

Bru. I am not Gamefome? I do lack fome part
Of that quick Spirit that is in *Antony :*
Let me not hinder *Caffius* your defires;
I'le leave you.

Caffi. Brutus, I do obferve you now of late :
I have not from your eyes, that gentlenefs
And fhew of love, as I was wont to have :
You bear too ftubborn, and fo ftrange a hand
Over your Friend, that loves you.

Bru. Caffius,
Be not deceiv'd ; If I have veil'd my look,
I turn the trouble of my Countenance
Meerly upon my felf. Vexed I am
Of late, with paffions of fome difference,
Conceptions only proper to my felf,
Which give fome foyl (perhaps) to my behaviour :
But let not therefore my good Friends be griev'd,
(Among which *Caffius* be you one)
Nor conftrue any further My neglect,
Then that poor *Brutus* with himfelf at War,
Forgets the fhews of Love to other men.

Caffi. Then *Brutus,* I have much miftook your paffion,
By means whereof, this Breaft of mine hath buried
Thoughts of great value, worthy Cogitations.
Tell me, good *Brutus,* can you fee your face ?

Bru. No *Caffius :*
For the eye fees not it felf but by reflection,
By fome other things.

Caffi. 'Tis juft,
And it is very much lamented, *Brutus,*
That you have no fuch Mirrors, as will turn
Your hidden worthinefs into your eye,
That you might fee your fhadow :
I have heard,
Where many of the beft refpect in *Rome,*
(Except immortal *Cæfar*) fpeaking of *Brutus,*
And groaning underneath this Ages yoak,
Have wifh'd, that Noble *Brutus* had his eyes.

Bru. Into what dangers, would you
Lead me *Caffius.*
That you would have me feek into my felf,

For that which is not in me?

    Cas. Therefore good *Brutus*, be prepar'd to hear:
And fince you know, you cannot fee your felf?
So well as by Reflection; I your Glafs,
Will modeftly difcover to your felf
That of your felf, which you yet know not of
And be not jealous on me, gentle *Brutus.*
Where I a common Laughter, or did ufe
To ftale with ordinary Oaths my love
To every new Protefter: If you know,
That I do fawn on men, and hugg them hard,
And after fcandal them: Or if you know
That I profefs my felf in Banquetting
To all the Rout, then hold me dangerous.

Flourifh and Shout.

    Bru. What means this Shouting?
I do fear, the People choofe *Cæfar*
For their King.
    Caffi. I, do you fear it?
Then muft I think you would not have it fo.
    Bru. I would not *Caffius*, yet I love him well:
But wherefore do you hold me here fo long?
What is it, that you would impart to me!
If it be ought toward the general Good,
Set Honour in one eye, and Death i'th' other
And I will look on both indifferently:
For let the Gods fo fpeed me, as I love
The name of Honour, more than I fear Death.
    Caffi. I know that vertue to be in you, *Brutus*,
As well as I do know your outward favour.
Well, Honour is the fubject of my Story:
I cannot tell, what you and other men
Think of this life; but for my fingle felf,
I had as lief not be, as live to be
In awe to fuch a thing, as I my felf.
I was born free as *Cæfar*, fo were you,
We both have fed as well, and we can both
Endure the Winters cold, as well as he,
For once upon a Raw and Gafty day,
The troubled *Tyber*, chafing with her Shores,
Cæfar faid to me, dar'ft thou *Caffius* now
Leap in with me in to this angry Flood,
And fwim to yonder Point? Upon the word,
Accounted as I was, I plunged in,

And

And bad him follow : fo indeed he did.
The Torrent roar'd, and we did buffet it
With lufty Sinews, throwing it afide,
And ftemming it with hearts of Controverfy.
But e'er we could arrive the Point propos'd,
Cæfar cry'd, Help me *Caffius*, or I fink.
I (as *Æneas*, our great Anceftor,
Did from the Flames of *Troy*, upon his fhoulder
The old *Anchifes* bear) fo from the waves of *Tyber*
Did I the tyred *Cæfar* : And this Man,
Is now become a God, and *Caffius* is
A wretched Creature, and muft bend his body,
If *Cæfar* carelefsly but nod on him.
He had a Feavour when he was in *Spain*,
And when the Fit was on him, I did mark
How he did fhake : 'Tis true, this God did fhake,
His Coward lips did from their Colour flye,
And that fame Eye, whofe bend doth awe the World,
Did lofe his Luftre : I did hear him groan :
I, and that Tongue of his, that bad the *Romans*
Mark him, and write his Speeches in their Books,
Alas, it cryed, give me fome drink *Titinius*,
As a fick Girl : Ye Gods, it doth amaze me,
A man of fuch a feeble temper fhould
So get the ftart of the Majeftick World,
And bear the Palm alone.

Shout. Florrifh.

Bru. Another general fhout ?
I do believe, that thefe Applaufes are
For fome new honours, that are heap'd on *Cæfar*.

Caff. Why man, he doth beftride the narrow World,
Like a *Coloffus*, and we petty men
Walk under his huge Legs, and peep about,
To find our felves difhonourable Graves.
Men at fome time, are Mafter of their Fates.
The fault (dear *Brutus*) is not in our Stars,
But in our felves, that we are Underlings,
Brutus and *Cæfar* : What fhould be in that *Cæfar* ?
Why fhould that Name be founded more than yours ?
Write them together : Yours is as fair a Name :
Sound them, it doth become the mouth as well.
Weigh them, it is as heavy : Conjure with 'em,
Brutus will ftart a Spirit as foon as *Cæfar*.
Now in the Names of all the Gods at once,
Upon what meat doth this our *Cæfar* feed,
That he is grown fo great ? Age, thou art afham'd.

Rome;

Rome, thou haft loft the breed of Noble Bloods.
When went there by an Age, fince the great Flood,
But it was fam'd with more then with one man ?
When could they fay (till now) that talk'd of *Rome*,
That her wide Walks incompaft but one man ?
Now is it *Rome* indeed, and *Rome* enough
When there is in it but one only man.
O ! you and I, have heard our Fathers fay,
There was a *Brutus* once, that would have brook'd
Th' eternal Devil to keep his State in *Rome*,
As eafily as a King.

 Bru. That you do love me, I am nothing jealous :
What you would work me too, I have fome aim :
How I have thought of this, and of thefe times,
I fhall recount hereafter. For this prefent,
I would not fo (with love I might intreat you)
Be any further mov'd : What you have faid
I will confider ; what you have to fay
I will with patience hear, and find a time
Both meet to hear, and anfwer fuch high things.
Till then my Noble Friend, chew upon this ;
Brutus had rather be a Villager,
Then to repute himfelf a Son of *Rome*
Under thefe hard Conditions, as this time
Is live to lay upon us.

 Caffi. I am glad that my weak words
Have ftruck but thus much fhew of fire from *Brutus*.

   Enter Cæfar *and his Train.*

 Bru. The Games are done,
And *Cæfar* is returning.

 Caffi. As they pafs by.
Pluck *Caska* by the Sleeve,
And he will (after his four fafhion) tell you
What hath proceeded worthy note to day.

 Bru. I will do fo : But look you *Caffius*,
The angry fpot doth glow on *Cæfar*'s brow,
And all the reft, look like a chidden Train ;
Calphurnia's Cheek is pale and *Cicero*
Looks with fuch ferret, and fuch fiery Eyes,
As we have feen him in the Capitol
Being croft in Conference, by fome Seneators.

 Caffi. *Caska* will tell us what the matter is.

 Cæf. *Antonio.*

 Ant. *Cæfar.*

 Cæf. Let me have men about me, that are fat,

     B

Sleek-headed men, and such as sleep a nights:
Yond *Cassius* has a lean and hungry look,
He thinks too much : such men are dangerous.
He is a Noble *Roman* and well given.

  Cæs. Would he were fatter ; but I fear him not :
Yet if my name were liable to fear,
I do not know the man I should avoid
So soon as that spare *Cassius*. He reads much,
He is a great Observer, and he looks
Quite through the deeds of men. He loves no Plays.
As thou dost *Antony* : he hears no Musick ;
Seldom he smiles, and smiles in such a sort,
As if he mock'd himself, and scorn'd his spirit
That could be mov'd to smile at any thing.
Such men as he be never at hearts ease,
While they behold a greater than themselves,
And therefore are they very dangerous.
I rather tell thee what is to be fear'd,
Than what I fear : for always I am *Cæsar*.
Come on my right hand, for this Ear is deaf,
And tell me truly, what thou think'st of him.   *Sennit.*
                Exeunt Cæsar *and his Train.*

  Cask. You pull me by the Cloak, would you speak with me ?
  Bru. I, *Caska*, tell us what hath chanc'd to day
That *Cæsar* looks so sad.
  Cask. Why you were with him, were you not ?
  Bru. I should not then have ask'd *Caska* what hath chanc'd.
  Cask. Why there was a Crown offer'd him ; and being offer'd
him, he put it by with the back of his hand thus, and then the
people fell a shouting.
  Bru. What was the second noise for ?
  Cask. Why for that too.
  Cassi. They shouted thrice. What was the last cry for ?
  Cask. Why for that too.
  Bru. Was the Crown offer'd him thrice ?
  Cask. I marry was't, and he put by thrice, every time gentler
than other, and at every putting by, mine honest Neighbours shouted.
  Cassi. Who offer'd him the Crown ?
  Cask. Why *Antony.*
  Bru. Tell us the manner of it, gentle *Caska.*
  Cask. I can as well be hang'd as tell the manner of it : It was meer
Foolery, I did not mark it. I saw *Mark Antony* offer him a Crown,
yet 'twas not a Crown neither, 'twas one of these Coronets ; and
as I told you he put it by once ; but for all that, to my thinking,
he would fain have had it. Then he offered it to him again ; then
                                                        he

he put it by again : But to my thinking, he was very loath to lay his fingers off it : And then he offered it the third time ; he put it the third time by ; and ſtill as he refus'd it, the rabblement howted, and clapp'd their chopt hands, and threw up their ſweaty Night-caps, and uttered ſuch a deal of ſtinking Breath, becauſe *Cæſar* refus'd the Crown, that it almoſt choaked *Cæſar* ; for he ſwoon-ded, and fell down at it. And for my own part, I durſt not laugh, for fear of opening my Lips, and receiving the bad Air.

Caſſi. But ſoft I pray you : what, did *Cæſar* ſwound ?

Cas. He fell down in the Market-place, and foam'd at mouth, and was ſpeechleſs.

Bru. 'Tis very like he hath the Falling-ſickneſs.

Cas. I know not what you mean by that, but I am ſure *Cæſar* fell down. If the tag-rag People did not clap him, and hiſs him, according as he pleas'd, and diſpleas'd them, as they uſe to do the Players in the Theatre. I am no true man.

Bru. What ſaid he, when he came unto himſelf ?

Cas. Marry, before he fell down, when he perceived the com-mon Herd was glad, he refuſed the Crown, he pluckt me one his Double, and offer'd them his Throat to Cut ; and had I been a man of any Occupation, if I would not have taken him at a word ; I would I might go to Hell among the Rogues, and ſo he fell. When he came to himſelf again, he ſaid, if he had done, or ſaid any thing amiſs, he deſired their Worſhips to think it was his Infirmity. Three or four Wenches where I ſtood, cryed, Alaſs ! good Soul, and forgave him with all their Hearts ; but there's no heed to be taken of them, if *Cæſar* had ſtabb'd their Mothers, they would have done no leſs.

Bru. And after that, he came thus ſad away.

Cas. I.

Caſſi. Did *Cicero* ſay any thing ?

Cas. I, he ſpoke Greek.

Caſſi. To what effect ?

Cas. Nay, and I tell you that, I'll ne'er look you i'th' face again. But thoſe that underſtood him, ſmil'd at one another, and ſhook their Heads ; but for my own part, it was Greek to me, I could tell you more News too : *Murrellus* and *Flavius*, for pulling Scarfs off *Cæſar's* Images, are put to ſilence. Fare you well. There was more Foolery yet, if I could remember it.

Caſſi. Will you ſup with me to Night, *Caska* ?

Cas. No, I am promis'd forth.

Caſſi. Will you dine with me to morrow ?

Cas. I, if I be alive, and your mind hold, and your Dinner worth the eating.

Caſſi. Good, I will expect you.

Cas.

Cas. Do fo : farewel both.   *Exit.*

Bru. What a blunt fellow is this grown to be ?
He was quick Mettle when he went to School.

Caſſi. So he is now, in execution
Of any hold, or Noble Enterprife,
However he puts on his tardy form :
This Ruddineſs is a Sawce to his good Wit,
Which gives men ſtomack to digeſt his words
With better Appetite.

Bru. And fo it is :
For this time I will leave you :·
To morrow, if you pleaſe to ſpeak with me,
I will come home to you ; or if you will,
Come home to me, and I will wait for you.

Caſſi. I will do ſo : tell then, think of the World.
                 Exit. Brutus.

Well *Brutus,* thou art Noble ; yet I ſee,
Thy Honourable Mettle may be wrought
From that it is diſpos'd : therefore it is meet,
That Noble minds keep ever with their likes :
For who ſo firm, that cannot be ſeduc'd ?
Cæſar doth bear me hard, but he loves *Brutus.*
If I where *Brutus* now, and he were *Caſſius,*
He ſhould humour me, I will this Night,
In ſeveral Hands, in at his Windows throw
As if they came from ſeveral Citizens,
Writings, all tending to the great opinion
That *Rome* holds of his Name, wherein obſcurely
Cæſar Ambition ſhall be glanced at.
And after this, let *Cæſar* ſet him ſure,
For we will ſhake him, or worſe days endure.
                 Exit.

       Thunder, and Lightning. Enter Caska,
            and Trebonius.

Treb. Good even, *Caska* ; brought you *Cæſar* home ?
Why are you breathleſs, and why ſtare you ſo ?

Cas. Are not you mov'd, when all the ſway of Earth
Shakes, like a thing unfirm ? O *Cicero,*
I have ſeen tempeſts, when the ſcolding Winds
Have riv'd thy knotty Oaks, and I have ſeen
Th' ambitious Ocean ſwell, and rage, and foam,
To be exalted with the threatning Clouds :
But never till to Night, never till now,
Did go through a Tempeſt-dropping-fire.
Either there is a Civil ſtrife in Heaven,

                         Or

Or elfe the World too fawcy with the Gods
Incenfes them to fend Deftruction.

   Treb. Why faw you any thing more wonderful?

   Cas. A common flave, you know him well by fight,
Held up his left Hand, which did flame and burn
Like twenty Torches join'd, and yet his Hand,
Not fenfible of fire, remain'd unfcorch'd.
Befides, I ha' not fince put up my Sword,
Againft the Capitol I met a Lyon,
Who gaiz'd upon me, and went furly by,
Without anoying me. And there were drawn
Upon a heap, a hundred gaftly Women,
Transform'd with their fear, who fwore, they faw
Men, all in fire, walk up and down the ftreets.
And yefterday, the Bird of Night did fit,
Even at Noon-day, upon the Market-place,
Howting, and fhreeking. When thefe Prodigies
Do fo conjoyntly meet, let not man fay
Thefe are their Reafons, they are Natural;
For I believe they are portentious things
Unto the Climate that they point upon.

   Treb. Indeed, it is a ftrange difpofed time:
But men may conftrue things after their fafhion.
Clean from the purpofe of the things themfelves.
Comes *Cæfar* to the Capitol to morrow?

   Cas. He doth, for he bid *Aotonio*
Send word to you, he would be there to morrow.

   Treb. Good-night then, *Caska:*
This difturbed Sky is not to walk in.

   Cas. Farewel *Trebonius.*   Exit *Cicero.*
                Enter Caffius.

   Caffi. Who's there?

   Cas. A *Roman.*

   Caffi. Caska, by your Voice.

   Cas. Your Ear is good.
Caffius, what Night is this?

   Caffi. A very pleafing Night to honeft men.

   Cas. Who ever knew the Heavens menace fo?

   Caffi. Thofe that have known the Earth fo full of faults.
For my part, I have walk'd about the ftreets,
Submiting me unto the perilous Night;
And thus embraced, *Caska,* as you fee,
Have bar'd my Bofom to the Thunder-ftone,
And when the crofs blue Lightning feem'd to open
The Breaft of Heaven, I did prefent my felf
Even in the aim, and very flafh of it.

                          Cas.

Cas. But wherefore did you ſo much tempt the Heavens?
It is the part of Men to fear and tremble,
When the moſt mighty Gods by Tokens ſend
Such dreadful Heralds to aſtoniſh us.

Caſſi. You are dull, *Caska:*
And thoſe ſparks of Life that ſhould be in a Roman,
You do want, or elſe you uſe not,
You look pale, and gaze, and put on fear,
And caſt your ſelf in wonder,
To ſee the ſtrange impatience of the Heavens:
But if you would conſider the true cauſe,
Why all theſe Fires, why all theſe gliding Ghoſts,
Why Birds and Beaſts, from quality and kind,
Why old Men, Fools, and Children calculate,
Why all theſe things change from their Ordinance,
Their Natures, and preformed Faculties,
To monſtrous quality; why you ſhall find,
That Heaven hath infus'd them with theſe Spirits,
To make them Inſtruments of fear and warning,
Upon ſome monſtrous State.
Now could I, *Caska,* name to thee a man,
Moſt like this dreadful Night,
That thunders, lightens, opens Graves, and roars,
As doth the Lion in the Capitol:
A man no mightier than thy ſelf, or me,
In perſonal Action; yet prodigious grown,
And fearful as theſe ſtrange Eruptions are.

Cas. 'Tis *Cæſar* that you mean:
Is it not, *Caſſius?*

Caſſi. Let it be who it is: for *Romans* now
Have Thewes and Limbs like to their Anceſtors;
But woe the while, our Fathers minds are dead,
And we are govern'd with our Mothers Spirits,
Our yoke and ſufferance ſhew us Womaniſh.

Cas. Indeed, they ſay, the Senators to morrow
Mean to eſtabliſh *Cæſar* as a King:
And he ſhall wear his Crown by Sea and Land,
In every place, ſave here in *Italy.*

Caſſi. I know where I will wear this Dagger then:
Caſſius from Bondage will deliver *Caſſius:*
Therein, ye Gods, you make the weak moſt ſtrong;
Therein, ye Gods, you Tyrants do defeat.
Nor ſtony Tower, nor Walls of beaten Braſs,
Nor airleſs Dungeon, nor ſtrong Links of Iron,
Can be re-tentive to the ſtrength of ſpirit:
But Life being weary of theſe worldly Bars,

Never

Never lacks power to difmifs it felf
If I know this, know all the World befides.
That part of Tyranny that I do bear,
I can fhake off at pleafure,   *Thunder ftill.*
    Cas. So can I :
So every Bond man in his own hand bears
The power to cancel his Captivity.
    Caffi. And why fhould *Cæfar* be a Tyrant then ?
Poor man, I know he would not be a Wolf,
But that he fees the *Romans* are but Sheep :
He were no Lyon, were not *Romans* Hinds.
Thofe that with haft will make a mighty fire.
Begin it with weak Straws. What trafh is *Rome ?*
What Rubbifh, and what Offal ? when it ferves
For the bafe matter, to illuminate
So vile a thing as *Cæfar.* But oh Grief,
Where haft thou led me ? I (perhaps) fpeak this
Before a willing Bondman : then I know
My anfwer muft be made. But I am arm'd,
And dangers are to me indifferent.
    Cas. You fpeak to *Caska,* and to fuch a man ;
That is no flearing Tell-tale. Hold, my Hand ;
Be factious for redrefs of all thefe Griefs,
And I will fet this foot of mine as far,
As who goes fartheft.
    Caffi. There's bargain made.
Now know you, *Caska,* I have mov'd already
Some certain of the Nobleft minded *Romans*
To undergo, with me, an Enterprize,
Of Honourable dangerous confequence ;
And I do know by this, they ftay for me
In *Pompey's* Porch ; for now this fearful Night,
There is no ftir, or walking in the ftreets ;
And the Complexion of the Element
Is Favours, like the Work we have in hand,
Moft bloody, fiery, and moft terrible.

              Enter Cinna.

    Cas. Stand clofe a while, for here comes one in haft.
    Caffi. 'Tis *Cinna :* I do know him by his Gate.
He is a Friend, *Cinna,* where haft you fo ?
    Cinna. To find out you ; Who's that, *Metellus Cymber ?*
    Caffi. No it is *Caska,* one incorporate
To our Attempts. Am I not ftay'd for, *Cinna ?*

                              Cinna.

Cinna. I am glad on't.
What a fearful Night is this?
There's two or three of us have seen ſtrange ſights.
Caſſi. Am I not ſtay'd for? tell me.
Cinna. Yes you are. O *Caſſius*,
If you could but win the Noble *Brutus*
To our party——
Caſſi. Be you content. Good *Cinna*, take this Paper,
And look you lay it in the Prætors Chair,
Where *Brutus* may but find it: and throw this
In at his Window; ſet this up with Wax
Upon old *Brutus* Statue: all this done,
Repair to *Pompey*'s Porch, where you ſhall find us.
Is *Decius Brutus* and *Trebonius* there?
Cinna. All, but *Metellus Cymber*, and he's gone
To ſeek you at your houſe. Well, I will hie,
And ſo beſtow theſe Papers as you bad me.
Caſſi. That done, repair to *Pompey*'s Theatre.
                                        Exit Cinna.
Come *Caska*, you and I will yet e're day,
See *Brutus* at his houſe; three parts of him
Is ours already, and the man entire
Upon the next encounter, yields him ours.
Cas. O, he ſits high in all the Peoples Hearts,
And that which would appear Offence in us,
His Countenance, like richeſt *Alchymy*,
Will change to Vertue and to Worthineſs.
Caſſi. Him, and his worth, and our great need of him
You have right well conceited: let us go,
For it is after Mid-night, and e're day,
We will awake him and be ſure of him:
                                        Exeunt.

Actus Secundus.

Enter Brutus *in his Orchard.*

Bru. What *Lucius*, ho.
I cannot, by the progreſs of the Stars,
Give gueſs how near to day *Lucius*, I ſay?
I would it were my fault to ſleep ſo ſoundly.
When, *Lucius*, when; awake, I ſay: what *Lucius.*
                                        Enter

Luc. Call'd you, my Lord ?

Bru. Get me a Taper in my Study, *Lucius* ;
When it is lighted come and call me here :

Luc. I will my Lord.   *Exit.*

Bru. It muſt be by his death : and for my part,
I know no perſonal cauſe, to ſpurn at him,
But for the general.   He would be Crown'd :
How that might change his nature, there's the queſtion ?
It is the bright day that brings forth the Adder,
And that craves wary walking : Crown him that,
And then I grant we put a Sting in him,
That at his will he may do danger with.
Th' abuſe of Greatneſs, is, when it disjoyns
Remorſe from Power : and to ſpeak truth of *Cæſar.*
I have not known, when his Affeƈtions ſway'd
More than his Reaſon.   But 'tis a common prɔof,
That Lowlineſs is young Ambition's Ladder.
Whereto the Climber upwards turns his Face :
But when he once attains the upmoſt Round,
He then unto the Ladder turns his Back,
Looks in the Clouds, ſcorning the baſe degrees
By which he did aſcend : ſo *Cæſar* may ;
Then leaſt he may, prevent.   And ſince the Quarrel
Will bear no colour, for the thing he is,
Faſhion it thus ; that what he is, augmented,
Would run to thoſe, and theſe extremities :
And there o'er think him as a Serpents Egg,
Which hatch'd, would as his kind grow miſchievous ;
And kill him in the ſhell.

Luc. The Taper burneth in your Cloſet, Sir :
Searching the Window for a Flint, I found
This paper, thus ſeal'd up, and I am ſure
It did not lye there when I went to Bed.

                    Gives him the Letter.

Bru. Get you to Bed again, it is not day :
Is not to morrow (Boy) the firſt of *March ?*

Luc. I know not Sir.

Bru. Look in the Galendar, and bring me word.

Luc. I will, Sir.   *Exit.*

Bru. The Exhalations whizzing in the air.
Give ſo much light, that I may read by them.

                    Opens the Letter and reads.

Brutus, *thou ſleep'ſt* ; *awake, and ſee thy ſelf.*
Shall Rome, *&c. ſpeak, ſtrike, redreſs,*

              C

Brutus, *thou fleep'ft* : *awake* ;
Such inftigations have been often dropt,
Where I have took them up :
Shall *Rome*, *&c.* Thus muft I piece it out,
Shall *Rome*, ftand under one mans awe? What *Rome?*
My Anceftors did from the ftreets of *Rome*,
The *Tarquin* drive, when he was call'd a King.
Speak, ftrike, redrefs. Am I entreated
To fpeak and ftrike? O *Roman*, I make the promife,
If the redrefs will follow, thou receiveft
Thy full Petition at the hand of *Brutus*.

Enter Lucius.

Luc. Sir, *March* is wafted Fifteen days.

·Knock within.

Bru. 'Tis good. Go to the gate, fome body knocks,
Since *Caffius* firft did whet me againft *Cæfar*,
I have not flept
Between the acting of a dreadful thing,
And the firft motion, all the *Interim* is
Like a *Phantafma*, or hideous Dream :
The *Genius*, and the mortal inftruments
Are then in council and the ftate of man,
Like to a little Kingdom, fuffers then
The nature of an Infurrection.

Enter Lucius.

Luc. Sir 'tis your Brother *Caffius* at the Door,
Who defires to fee you.

Bru. Is he alone?

Luc. No, Sir, there are more with him.

Bru. Do you know them?

Luc. No, Sir, there Hats are pluckt about their Ears,
And half their Faces buried in their Cloacks,
That by no means I may difcover them,
By any mark of favour.

Bru. Let 'em enter :
They are the Faction O Confpiracy,
Sham'ft thou to fhew thy dang'rous Brow by Night,
When evils are moft free? O them by day,
Where wilt thou find a Cavern dark enough,
To mask thy monftrous Vifage? feek no Confpiracy,
Hide it in Smiles, and Affability :

For

For thou hath thy Native semblance on,
Not *Erebus* it self were dim enough,
To hide thee from prevention.

Enter the Conspirators, Caffius, Caska, Decius, Cinna,
Metellus and Trebonius.

Caff. I think we are too bold upon your Reft :
Good morrow *Brutus,* do we trouble you ?
Bru. I have been up this Hour, awake all Night :
Know I thefe men, that come along with you ?
Caff. Yes, every man of them ; and no man here
But honours you : and every one doth wifh,
You had but that opinion of your felf,
Which every Noble *Roman* bears of you,
This is *Trebonius.*
Bru. He is welcome hither.
Caff. This *Decius Brutus.*
Bru. He is welcome too.
Caff. This *Caska*; this, *Cinna*; and this *Metellus Cymber.*
Bru. They are all welcome.
What watchful Cares do interpofe themfelves
Betwixt your Eyes and Night ?
Caff. Shall I intreat a word ?   *They whifper.*
Decius. Here lies the Eaft ; doth not the Day break here?
Cas. No.
Cin. O pardon, Sir, it doth, and yon gray Lines,
That fret the Clouds, are Meffengers of Day.
Cas. You fhall confefs, that you are both deceiv'd ?
Here, as I point my Sword, the Sun arifes,
Which is a great way growing on the South,
Weighing the youthful Seafon of the Year,
Some two Months hence, up higher toward the North
He firft prefents his Fire, and the high Eaft
Stands as the Capitol, directly here.
Bru. Give me your hands all over, one by one.
Caff. And let us fwear our Refolution.
Bru. No, not an Oath; if not the Face of men,
The Sufferance of our Souls, the times Abufe ;
If thefe Motives weak, break off betimes,
And every Man hence to his idle Bed ?
So let high-fighted Tyranny range on,

C 2   Till

Till each Man drop by Lottery, But if thefe
(As I am fure they do) bear Fire enough
To kindle Cowards, and to fteal with Valour
The melting Spirits of Woman.   Then Countrymen,
What need we any Spur, but our own Caufe,
To prick us to redrefs ? What other Bond,
Than fecret *Romans*, that have fpoke the Word,
And will not palter ? And what other Oath
Than Honefty to honefty engag'd,
That this fhall be, or we fhall fall for it.
Swear Priefts and Cowards, and Men cautelous
Old feedle Carrions and fuch fuffering Souls
That welcome Wrongs : Unto bad Caufes fwear,
Such Creatures as Men doubt ; but do not ftain
The even vertue of our Enterprize,
Nor th' infuppreffive mettle of our Spirits,
To think, that, or our Caufe, or our Performance
Did need an Oath.   When every drop of Blood
That every *Roman* bears, and Nobly bears,
Is guilty of a feveral Baftardy,
If he do break the fmalleft Particle
Of any Promife that hath paft from him.
 Cef. But what of *Cicero ?* Shall we found him ?
I think he will ftand very ftrong with us.
 Cask. Let us not leave him out.
 Cin. No by no means.
 Metel. O let us have him ! for his filver Hairs
Will purchafe a good opinion :
And by Mens Voices, to commend our Deeds :
It fhall be faid his Judgment rul'd our Hands,
Our Youths and Wildnefs fhall no whit appear,
But all be buried in his Gravity.
 Bru. O name him not ; let us not break with him
For he will never follow any thing
That other men begin.
 Caffi. Then leave him out.
 Cask. Indeed, he is not fit.
 Decius. Shall no man elfe be touch'd, but only *Cæfar ?*
 Caffi. *Decius* well urg'd : I think it is not meet,
Mark Antony, fo well belov'd of *Cæfar.*
Should out-live *Cæfar*, we fhall find of him
A fhrewd Contriver.   And you know, his means,
If he improve them, may well ftretch fo far
As to annoy us all : which to prevent,
Let *Antony* and *Cæfar* fall together.

Bru. Our Courſe will ſeem too bloody, *Caius Caſſius,*
To cut the Head off, and then hack the Limbs:
Like Wrath in Death, and Envy afterwards:
For *Antony* is but a Limb of *Cæſar,*
Let's be Sacraficers, but no Butchers, *Caius* :
We all ſtand up againſt the Spirite of *Cæſar,*
And in the Spirit of Men there is no Blood
O that we then could come by *Cæſar's* Spirit,
And not diſmember *Cæſar* ! But (alaſs !)
Cæſar muſt bleed for it.   And gentle Friends,
Let's kill him boldly, but not wrathfully :
Let's carve him, as a Diſh fit for the Gods,
Not hew him as a Carkaſs fit for Hounds ;
And let our Hearts, as ſubtle Maſters do,
Stir up their Servants to an act of Rage,
And after ſeem to chide 'em.   This ſhall make
Our purpoſe neceſſary, and not envious.
With ſo appearing to the common Eyes,
We ſhall be call'd Purgers, not Murtherers.
And for *Mark Antony,* think not of him :
For he can do no more than *Cæſar's* Arm,
When *Cæſar's* Head is off.
    Caſſi. Yet I fear him,
For in the ingrafted Love he bears to *Cæſar.*
    Bru. Alas ! good *Caſſius,* do not think of him :
If he love *Cæſar,* all that he can do
Is to himſelf ; take thought, and dye for *Cæſar* ;
And that were much he ſhould ; for he is given
To Sports and Wildneſs, and much company.
    Treb. There is no fear in him ; let him not dye,
For he will live and laugh at this hereafter.
                                        Clock ſtrikes.

    Bru. Peace, count the Clock.
    Caſſi. The Clock hath ſtricken three.
    Treb. 'Tis time to part.
    Caſſi. But it is doubtful yet,
Whether *Cæſar* will come forth to day, or no :
For he is Superſtitious grown of late,
Quite from the main Opinion he held once,
Of Fantaſie, of Dreams, and Ceremonies :
It may be theſe apparent Prodigies,
The unaccuſtom'd Terror of this Night ;
And the Perſwaſion of his Augurers,
May hold from the Capitol to day.
    Decius. Never fear that : if he be ſo reſolv'd,
I can o'erſway him : For he loves to hear,

                                        That

That Unicorns may be betray'd with Trees,
And Bears with Glaſſes, Elephants with Holes,
Lions with Toils, and Men with Flatterers,
But when I tell him he hates Flatterers,
He ſays, he does; begin then moſt flattered.
Let me work:
For I can give his Humour the true bent;
And I will bring him to the Capitol.

    Caſſi. Nay, we will all of us be there to fetch him.
    Bru. By the eighth Hour, is that the uttermoſt?
    Cin. Be that the uttermoſt, and fail not then.
    Met. Caius Ligarius doth bear *Cæfar* hard,
Who rated him for ſpeaking well of *Pompey,*
I wonder none of you have thought of him.
    Bru. Now good *Metellus* go along by him.
He loves me well, and I have given him Reaſon,
Send him but hither, and I'll faſhion him.
    Caſſi. The Morning comes upon's:
We'll leave you, *Brutus,*
And Friends diſperſe your ſelves; but all remember
What you have ſaid, and ſhew your ſelves true *Romans.*
    Bru. Good Gentlemen look freſh and merrily.
Let not our Looks put on our Purpoſes,
But bear it as our *Roman* Actors do.
With untir'd Spirits, and formal Conſtancy,
And ſo good Morrow to you every one.   *Exeunt.*

Manet Brutus.

Boy: *Lucius,* Faſt aſleep? It is no Matter.
Enjoy the honey-heavy dew of Slumber:
Thou haſt no Figures, nor no Fantaſies,
Which buſie Care draws in the Brains of Men;
Therefore thou ſleep'ſt ſo found.

Enter Portia.

    Por. Brutus; my Lord,
    Bru. Portia What mean you? wherefore riſe you now!
It is not for your Health, thus to commit
Your weak Condition to the raw cold Morning.
    Por. Nor for yours neither. Y'have ungently, *Brutus*
Stole from my Bed: and yeſternight at Supper
You ſuddenly aroſe, and walk'd about,
Muſing and ſighing, with your Arms a-croſs;
And when I asq'd you what the Matter was,
You ſtar'd upon me with ungentle Looks.
I urg'd you further; then you ſcratch'd your Head,

                                 And

And too impatiently ftamp'd with your Foot :
Yet I infifted ; yet you anfwer'd not,
But with an angry wafter of your hand,
Gave fign for me to leave you ; So I did,
Fearing to ftrengthen that Impatience
Which feem'd too much inkindled ; and withal
Hoping it was but an effect of Humour,
Which fometime hath his Hour with every Man.
It will not let you eat, nor talk, nor fleep ;
And cou'd it work fo much upon your Shape,
As it hath much prevail'd on your Condition,
I fhould not know you, *Brutus*, Dear my Lord,
Make me acquainted with your caufe of Grief.

 Bru. I am not well in Health, and that is all.

 Por. *Brutus* is wife, and were he not in Health,
He would embrace the means to come by it.

 Bru. Why fo I do : good *Portia* go to bed.

 Por. Is *Brutus* fick ? And is it Phyfical
To walk unbraced, and fuck up the Humours
Of the dark Morning ? What is *Brutus* fick ?
And will he fteel out of his wholefome bed
To dare the vile Contagion of the Night ?
·And tempt the rheumy and unpurged Air,
To add unto his Sicknefs ? No, my *Brutus*,
You have fome fick Offence within your Mind..
Which by the right and vertue of my place,
I ought to know of : And upon my knees,
I charm you by my once commended Beauty,
By all your Vows of Love, and that great Vow
Which did incorporate and make us one,
That you unfold to me, your felf, your half,
Why you are heavy, and what Men to night
Have had Refort to you ; for here have been
Some fix or feven, who did hide their Faces
Even from Darknefs.

 Bru. Kneel not, gentle *Portia.*

 Por. I fhould not need, if you were gentle *Brutus.*
Within the Bond of Marriage, tell me *Brutus,*
Is it expected, I fhould know no Secrets
That appertain to you ? Am I your felf,
But as it were in fort, or Limitation ?
To keep with you at Meals, comfort your Bed,·
And talk to you fometime ? Dwell I but in Suburbs
Of your good Pleafure ? If it be no more,
Portia is *Brutus* Harlot, not his Wife.

Bru. You

Bru. You are my true and honourable Wife,
As dear to me as are the ruddy Drops
That visit my sad Heart.

    Por. If this were true, then should I know this Secret.
I grant I am a Woman ; but withal,
A Woman that Lord *Brutus* took to Wife :
I grant I am a Woman ; but withal,
A Woman well reputed : *Cato*'s Daughter.
Think you, I am no stronger than my Sex ;
Being so father'd,. and so husbanded ?
Tell me your Counsels, I will not disclose 'em :
I have made strong Proof of my Constancy,
Giving my self a voluntary Wound
Here in the Thigh : Can I bear that with Patience,
And not my Husband's Secrets ?

    Bru. O ye Gods !
Render me worthy of this noble Wife.   *Knock.*
Hark, hark. one knocks : *Portia* go in a while,
And by and by thy Bosom shall partake
The Secrets of my Heart.
All my Engagements I will construe to thee,
All the Charactery of my sad Brows,
Leave me with haste.   *Exit Portia.*

       Enter Lucius *and* Ligarius.

    Lucius. Who's that knocks ?
    Luc. Here is a sick Man that wou'd speak with you.
    Bru. Caius Ligarius that *Metellus* spake of.
Boy, stand aside. *Caius Ligarius*, how ?
    Cai. Vouchsafe good Morrow from a feeble To gue.
    Bru. O what a time have you chose out, brave *Caius.*
To wear a Kerchief? Would you were not sick.
    Cai. I am not sick if *Brutus* have in hand
Any Exploit worthy the Name of Honour.
    Bru. Such an Exploit have I in hand, *Ligarius*,
Had you a healthful Ear to hear of it.
    Cai. By all the Gods that *Romans* bow before,
I here discard my sickness. Soul of *Rome*,
Brave Son, deriv'd from honourable Loins,
Thou like an Exorcist, hast conjur'd up
My mortified Spirits. Now bid me run,
And I will strive with things impossible,
Yea get the better of them. What's to do ?
    Bru. A piece of Work,
That will make sick Men whole.

                     Cai. But

Cai. But are not fome whole, that we muſt make fick?

Bru. That muſt we alſo. What it is, my *Caius*,
I ſhall unfold to thee, as we are going,
To whom it muſt be done.

Cai. Set on your Foot.
And with a Heart new-fir'd, I follow you,
To do I know not what: but it ſufficeth,
That *Brutus* leads me on.   *Thunder.*

Bru. Follow me then,   *Exeunt.*

Thunder and Lightening.

Enter Julius Cæſar *in his Night-gown.*

Cæſ. Nor Heaven nor Earth,
Have been at peace to night:
Thrice hath *Calphurnia* in her ſleep cry'd out;
Help, ho: They murther *Cæſar.* Who's within?

Enter a Servant.

Ser. My Lord.

Caſ. Go bid the Prieſts do preſent Sacrifice,

Ser. I will, my Lord.   *Exit.*

Enter Calphurnia.

Cal. What mean you *Cæſar*, think you to walk forth?
You ſhall not ſtir out of your houſe to day.

Cæſ. Cæſar, ſhall forth; the things that threaten'd me,
Ne'er look'd but on my Back: When they ſhall ſee
The Face of *Cæſar*, they are vaniſhed.

Cal. Cæſar, I never ſtood on Ceremonies,
Yet now they fright me: There is one within,
Beſides the things that we have heard and ſeen,
Recounts moſt horrid Sights ſeen by the Watch,
A Lioneſs hath whelped in the Street,
And Graves have yawn'd and yielded up their dead.
Fierce fiery Warriours fight upon the Clouds
In Ranks and Squadrons, and right form of War,
Which drizel'd Blood upon the Capitol:
The noiſe of Battle hurtled in the Air;
Horſes do neigh, and dying Men did groan,
And Ghoſts did ſhriek and ſqueal about the Streets.
O *Cæſar*, theſe things are beyond all uſe,
And I do fear them.

Cæſar. What can be avoided.
Whoſe End is purpos'd by the mighty Gods?
Yet *Cæſar* ſhall go forth: for theſe Predictions
Are to the World in general as to *Cæſar*.

Cal. When beggars dye, there are no Comets feen,
The Heavens themfelves blaze forth the Death of Princes.

Cæf. Cowards dye many times before their Deaths,
The valiant never tafte of Death but once.
Of all the wonders that I yet have heard,
It feems to me moft ftrange that Men fhould fear,
Seeing that Death, a neceffary End,
Will come when it will come.

     Enter a Servant.

What fay the Augures ?
 Ser. They wou'd not have you to ftir forth to day.
Plucking the Intrails of an Offering forth,
They could not find a Heart within the beaft.
 Cæf. The Gods do this in fhame of Cowardife :
Cæfar fhould be a Beaft without Heart
If he fhould ftay at home to day for fear ;
No, *Cæfar* fhall not ; Danger knows full well
That *Cæfar* is more dangerous then he.
We hear two Lions litter'd in one day.
And I the elder and more terrible,
And *Cæfar* fhall go forth.
 Cal. Alafs my Lord,
Your Wifdom is confum'd in Confidence :
Do not go forth to day : call it my Fear
That keeps you in the Houfe, and not your own.
We'll fend *Mark Antony* to the Senate-houfe,
And he fhall fay, you are not well to day :
Let me upon my knee prevail in this.
 Cæf. *Mark Antony* fhall fay I am not well,
And for thy Humour I will ftay at Home.

     Enter Decius.

Here's *Decius Brutus* he fhall tell them fo.
 Dec. Cæfar, all hail : Good morrow worthy *Cæfar*,
I come to fetch you to the Senate-houfe.
 Cæf. And you are come in very happy time,
To bear my greeting to the Senators,
And tell them that I will not come to day :
Cannot, is falfe, and that I dare not, falfer :
I will not come to day, tell them fo *Decius*.
 Cal. Say he is fick.
 Cæf. Shall *Cæfar* fend a Lye ?
Have I in Conqueft ftretch'd mine Arms fo far,
To be afraid to tell Gra beards the Truth ;
Decius, go tell 'hem, *Cæfar* will not come.
 Dec. Moft mighty *Cæfar* ; let me now fome caufe,

Left I be laugh'd at when I tell them fo.

Cæf. The Caufe is in my will, I will not come,
That is enough to fatisfie the Senate.
But for your private Satisfaction,
Becaufe I love you I will let you know.
Calphurnia, here my Wife ftays me at home :
She dream'd to night fhe faw my Statue,
Which like a Fountain, with an hundred Spouts,
Did run pure Blood ; and many lufty *Romans.*
Came fmiling, and did bath their Hands in it ;
And thefe does fhe apply, for Warnings and Portents,
And Evils imminent ; and on her knee
Hath begg'd that I will ftay at home to day.

Dec. This Dream is all amifs interpreted ;
It was a Vifion fair and fortunate ;
Your Statue fpouting Blood in many Pipes,
In which fo many fmiling *Romans* bath'd,
Signifies, that from you great *Rome* fhall fuck
Reviving Blood, and that great Man fhall prefs
For Tinctures, Stains, Reliques, and Cognifance.
This by *Calphurnia*'s Dream is fignified.

Cæf. And this way have you well expounded it ?

Dec. I have, when you have heard what I can fay.
And know it now, the Senate have concluded
To give this day a Crown to mighty *Cæfar.*
If you fhall fend the word you will not come,
Their minds may change. Befides it were a mock
Apt to be render'd, for fome one to fay,
Break up the Senate till another time.
When *Cæfar*'s Wife fhall meet with better Dreams.
If *Cæfar* hide himfelf, fhall they not whifper,
Lo *Cæfar* is afraid ?
Pardon me *Cæfar,* for my dear, dear Love
To your Proceedings, bids me tell you this :
And Reafon to my Love is liable.

Cæf. How foolifh do your Fears feem now *Calphurnia ?*
I am afhamed I did yield to them.
Give me my Robe, for I will go.

Enter Brutus, Ligarius, Metellus, Caska, Trebonius, Cinna, *and*
Publius.

And look where *Publius* is come to fetch me.

Pub. Good morrow, *Cæfar.*

Cæf. Welcome *Publius.*

What *Brutus,* are you ftirr'd fo early too ?
Good morrow, *Caska; Caius Ligarius,*

Cæfar was ne'er fo much your Enemy,
As that fame Ague which hath made you lean,
What is't a Clock ?

Bru *Cæfar*, 'tis ſtrucken Eight.

Cæf. I thank you for your Pains and Courtefie.

Enter Antony.

See, *Antony* that Revels long a nights
Is notwithſtanding up.   Good morrow *Antony.*

Ant. So to moſt Noble *Cæfar.*

Cæf. Bid them prepare within :
I am too blame to be thus waited for,
Now *Cinna*, now *Metellus*; what *Trebonius.*
I have an hours talk in ſtore for you ;
Remember that you call on me to day ;
Be near me, that I may remember you.

Treb. *Cæfar* I will ; and fo near will I be,
That your beſt Friends ſhall wiſh I had been farther.

Cæf. Good Friends go in, and taſte fome Wine with me.
And we (like Friends) will ſtraight way go together.

Bru. That every like is not the fame, O *Cæfar*,
The Heart of *Brutus* earns to think upon.   *Exeunt.*

Enter Artimedorus.

Cæfar. *beware of* Brutus, *take heed of* Caſſius, *come not
near* Caska, *have an eye to* Cinna, *truſt not* Trebonius, *mark
well* Metellus Cymber, Decius Brutus *loves thee not : Thou
haſt wrong'd* Caius Ligarius. *There is but one Mind in all
thefe Men, and it is bent againſt* Cæfar : *If thou beeſt not immortal, look about you, Security gives way to Conſpiracy, The
mighty Gods defend the.*   Thy Love, *Artimedorus.*
Here will I ſtand till *Cæfar* paſs along,
And as a Suiter will I give him this :
My Heart laments, the Virtue cannot live
Out of the Teeth of Emulation
If thou read this, O *Cæfar*, thou mayeſt live,
If not, the Fates which Traitors do contrive.   *Exit.*

Enter Portia *and* Lucius.

Por. I Prithee Boy, run to the Senate-houfe,

Say

Stay not to anfwer me, but get thee gone,
Why doeft thou ftay ?
   Luc. To know my Errand, Madam.
   Por. I would have had thee there and here again
'Ere I can tell thee what thou fhould'ft do there :
O Conftancy, be ftrong upon my fide,
Set a huge Mountain 'tween my Heart and Tongue :
I have a Mans Mind, but a Womans Might :
How hard it is for Woman to keep Counfel.
Art thou here yet ?
   Luc. Madam, what fhall I do ?
Run to the Capitol, and nothing elfe ?
And fo return to You, and nothing elfe ?
   Por. Yes, bring me word Boy, if my Lord looks well,
For he went fickly forth : and take good note
What *Cæfar* doth, what Suiters prefs to him.
Hark Boy, what noife is that ?
   Luc. I hear none, Madam.
   Por. Prithee liften well :
I heard a bufsling Rumour like a Fray,
And the Wind brings it from the Capitol,
   Luc. Madam, I hear nothing.

        Enter the Soothfayer.
   Por. Come hither Fellow, which way haft thou been ?
   Sooth. At mine own Houfe, good Lady.
   Por. What is't a Clock ?
   Sooth. About the ninth hour, Lady.
   Por. Is *Cæfar* yet gone to the Capitol ?
   Sooth. Madam, not yet, I go to take my Stand,
To fee him pafs on to the Capitol ?
   Por. Thou haft fome Suit to *Cæfar*, haft thou not ?
   Sooth. That I have, Lady, if it will pleafe *Cæfar*
To be fo good *Cæfar*, as to hear me :
I fhall befeech him to befriend himfelf.
   Por. Why know'ft thou any harms intended towards him ?
   Sooth. None that I know will be,
Much that I fear may chance :
Good morrow to you ; here the ftreet is narrow ;
The throng that follows *Cæfar* at the heels,
Of Senators, of Prætors, common Suiters,

                         Will

Will crowd a feeble man almoſt to death ;
I'll get me to a place more void, and there
Speak to great *Cæſar* as he comes along.   *Exit.*

   Par. I muſt go in.
Aye me, How weak a thing.
The Heart of Woman is, O *Brutus,*
The Heavens ſpeed thee in thine Enterprize.
Sure the Boy heard me ; *Brutus* hath a ſuit
That *Cæſar* will not grant, O, I grow faint ;
Run *Julius,* and commend me to my Lord,
Say I am merry ; Come to me again,
And bring me word what he doth ſay to thee.   *Exeunt.*

Actus Tertius.

        Flouriſh.

Enter Cæſar, Brutus, Caſſius, Caska, Decius, Metellus, Trebonius, Cinna, Antony, Lepidus, Artimedorus, Publius,
and the Soothſayer.

   Cæſ. The *Ides* of *March* are come.
   Sooth. I *Cæſar,* but not gone.
   Art. Hail *Cæſar* ; Read this Schedule.
   Dec. Trebonius doth deſire you to o'er-read
At your beſt leiſure, this his humble ſuit.
   Art. O *Cæſar,* read mine firſt ; for mine's a ſuit
That touches *Cæſar* nearer, Read it great *Cæſar.*
   Cæſ. What touches our ſelf, ſhall be laſt ſerv'd.
   Art. Delay not *Cæſar,* read it inſtantly.
   Pub. Sirrah, give place.
   Caſſi. What urge you your Petitions in the Street ?
Come to the Capitol.
   Popil. I wiſh your Enterprize to day may thrive.
   Caſſi. What Enterprize, *Popilius* ?
   Popil. Fare you well.
   Bru. What ſaid *Popilius Lena* ?
   Caſſi. He wiſh'd to day our Enterprize might thrive ;
I fear our Purpoſe is diſcovered.
   Bru. Look how he makes to *Cæſar* ; mark him.

                                         Caſſi.

Caſſi. Caska be ſudden, for we fear Prevention.
Brutus, what ſhall be done ? if this be known,
Caſſius or *Cæſar* never ſhall turn back,
For I will ſlay my ſelf.

    Bru. Caſſius be conſtant :
Popilius Lena, ſpeaks out of our Purpoſes,
For look he ſmiles, and *Cæſar* doth not change.

    Caſſi. Trebonius knows his time ; *Brutus,*
He draws *Mark Antony* out of the way.

    Dec. Where is *Metellus Cymber,* let him go,
And preſently prefer his ſuit to *Cæſar.*

    Bru. He is addreſt : preſs near, and ſecond him.

    Cin. Caska, you are the firſt that rears your hand.

    Caſſi. Are we all ready ; what is now amiſs,
That *Cæſar* and his Senate muſt redreſs ?

    Metel. Moſt high, moſt mighty, and moſt puiſſant *Cæſar,*
Metellus Cymber throws before thy Seat
An humble Heart.

    Cæſ. I muſt prevent thee *Cymber* :
Theſe Couchings, and theſe lowly Courtiers
Might fire the Blood of ordinary Men,
And turn pre-Ordinance, and firſt Decree,
Into the Lane of Children. Be not fond
To think that *Cæſar* bears ſuch Rebel blood
That will be thaw'd from the true Quality
With that which melteth Fools, I mean ſweet words,
Low-crooked Courteſies, and baſe Spaniel Fawning :
Thy Brother by decree is baniſhed.
If thou doſt bend, and pray, and fawn for him,
I ſpurn the like a Cur out of my way :
Know, *Cæſar* doth not wrong, nor without cauſe
Will he be ſatisfied.

    Metel. Is there no Voice more worthy than my own.
To ſound more ſweetly in great *Cæſar*'s Ear,
For the repealing of my baniſh'd Brother.

    Bru. I kiſs thy Hand, but not in Flattery *Cæſar* :
Deſiring thee that *Publius Cymber* may
Have an immediate freedom of Repeal.

    Cæſ. What *Brutus* ?

    Caſſi. Pardon *Cæſar, Cæſar* pardon ;
As low as to thy foot doth *Caſſius* fall,
To beg infranchiſement for *Publius Cimber.*

    Cæſ. I could be well mov'd, if I were as you,
If I could pray to move, Prayers would move me :
But I am conſtant as the Northern Star,
Of whoſe true fixt, and reſting quality,

There

There is no fellow in the Firmament.
The Skies are painted with unnumbred Sparks,
They are all Fire, and every one doth fhine :
But, there's but one in all doth hold his place. ·
So, in the World ; 'tis furnifh'd well with Men,
And Men are Flefh and Blood, and apprehenfive :
Yet in the number, I do know but One
That unaffaylable holds on his Rank,
Unfhak'd of Motion : and that I am he,
Let me a little fhew it, even in this :
That I was conftant *Cymber* fhould be banifh'd,
And conftant do remain to keep him fo.

 Cinna. O *Cæfar.*
 Cnf. Hence : Wilt thou lift up *Olympus* ?
 Decius. Great *Cæfar.*
 Cæf. Doth not *Brutus* bootlefs kneel ?
 Cask. Speak hands for me.

       They ftab Cæfar.
 Cæf. Et tu Brute ?----Then fall *Cæfar.* *Dies.*
 Cin. Liberty, freedom ; Tyrany is dead,
Run hence, proclaim, cry it about the Streets.
 Caffi. Some to the common Pulpits, and cry out
Liberty, Freedom, and Enfranchifement.
 Bru. People and Senators, be not affrighted:
Fly not, ftand ftill : Ambitions debt is paid.
 Cask. Go to the Pulpit, *Brutus.*
 Dec. And *Caffius* too.
 Bru. Where's *Publius ?*
 Cin. Here, quite confounded with this Mutiny.
 Met. Stand faft together, left fome Friend of *Cæfar*'s fhould charge.
 Bru. Talk not of ftanding. *Publius* good cheer,
There is no harm intended to your Perfon,
Nor to no *Roman* elfe ; fo tell them *Publius.*
 Caffi. And leave us *Publius,* left that the people
Rufhing on us, fhould do your Age fome mifchief.
 Bru. Do fo, and let no man abide this deed,
But we the Doers.

     Enter Trebonius

 Caffi. Where is *Antony ?*
 Treb. Fled to his Houfe amaz'd :
Men, Wives, and Children, ftare, cry out, and run,
As it were Doomfday.
 Bru. Fates, we will know your pleafures ;
That we fhall dye we know, 'tis but the time

            And

And drawing days out, that Men ftand upon.

Cask. Why he that cuts of twenty years of life,
Cuts off fo many years of fearing death.

Bru. Grant that, and then is death a benefit :
So are we *Cæfar*'s Friends, that have abridg'd
His time of fearing death.   Stoop *Romans*, ftoop,
And let us bath our hands in *Cæfar*'s blood
Up to the Elbows, and befmear our Swords :
Then walk we forth into the Market-place,
And waving our red Weapons o're our Heads,
Let's all cry Peace, Freedom, and Liberty.

Caffi. Stoop then, and wafh.   How many Ages hence
Shall this our lofty Scene be acted over,
In State unborn, and Accents yet unknown ?

Bru. How many times fhall *Cæfar* bleed in fport ?
That now on *Pompey*'s Bafis lye along,
No worthyer then the duft ?

Caffi. So oft as that fhall be,
So often fhall the knot of us be call'd,
The Men that gave their Country Liberty.

Dec. What, fhall we forth ?

Caffi. I, every Man away.
Brutus fhall lead, and we will grace his heels
With the moft boldeft, and beft hearts of *Rome.*

Enter a Servant.

Bru. Soft, who comes here ?   A Friend of *Antonys.*

Ser. Thus *Brutus* did my Mafter bid me kneel ;
Thus did *Mark Antony* bid me fall down,
And being proftrate, thus he bid me fay :
Brutus is Noble, Wife, Valiant, and Honeft ;
Cæfar was mighty, Bold, Royal, and Loving :
Say, I love *Brutus*, and I honour him ;
Say, I fear'd *Cæfar*, honour'd him, and lov'd him.
If *Brutus* will vouchfafe, that *Antony*
May fafely come to him, and be refolv'd
How *Cæfar* hath deferv'd to lye in death,
Mark Antony fhall not love *Cæfar* dead
So well as *Brutus* living ; but will follow
The Fortunes and Affairs of Noble *Brutus*,
Through the hazards of this untrod State,
With all true Faith.   So fays my Mafter *Antony.*

Bru. Thy Mafter is a Wife Valiant *Roman*,
I never thought him worfe.:
Tell him, fo pleafe him come unto this place.

E   He

He fhall be fatisfied : and by my Honour
Depart untouch'd :
　Ser. I'le fetch him prefently.　　　　　*Exit Servant.*
　Bru. I know that we fhall have him well to Friend.
　Caff. I wifh we may : But yet have I a mind
That fears him much : and my mifgiving ftill
Falls fhrewdly to the purpofe.

Enter Antony.

　Bru. But here comes *Antony.*
Welcome *Mark Antony.*
　Ant. O mighty *Cæfar* ! Doft thou lye fo low ?
Are all Conquefts, Glories, Triumphs, Spoils,
Shrunk to this little Meafure ? Fare thee well.
I know not Gentlemen what you intend,
Who elfe muft be let blood, who elfe is rank :
If I my felf, there is no hour fo fit,
As *Cæfar*'s death hour ; nor no Inftrument
Of half that worth, as thofe your Swords ; made rich
With the moft noble blood of all this World.
I do befeech yee, if you bear me hard,
Now, whil'ft your purpled hand do reek and fmoak,
Fulfil your pleafure. Live a Thoufand years,
I fhall not find my felf fo apt to dye.
No place will pleafe me fo, no mean of death,
As here by *Cæfar*, and by you cut off,
The Choice and Mafter Spirits of this Age.
　Bru. O *Antony* ! Beg not your death of us :
Though now we muft appear bloody and cruel,
As by our Hands, and this our prefent act
You fee we do : Yet fee you but our hands,
And this, the bleeding Bufinefs they have done,
Our hearts you fee not, they are pittiful.
And pitty to the general wrong to *Roman,*
As fire drives out fire, fo pitty, pitty
Hath done this deed on *Cæfar* : for your part,
To you, our Swords hath leaden points *Mark Antony* :
Our Arms in ftrength of malice, and our hearts
Of brothers temper, do receive you in,
With all kind love, good thoughts and reverence.
　Caff. Your voice fhall be as ftrong as any mans,
In the difpofing of new Dignities.
　Bru. Only be patient, till we have appeas'd
The Multitude, befide themfelves with fear,
And then we will deliver you the caufe,

Why

Why I, that did love *Cæsar* when I ftrook him,
Have thus proceeded.

 Ant. I doubt not of your Wifdom.
Let each man render me his bloody hand,
Firft *Marcus Brutus* will I fhake with you ;
Next *Caius Caffius* do I take your hand ;
Now *Decius Brutus* yours ? now yours *Metellus* ;
Yours *Cinna* ; and my valiant *Caska,* yours ;
Though laft, not leaft in love, yours good *Trebonius,*
Gentlemen all : Alas, what fhall I fay ?
My credit now ftands on fuch flippery ground,
That one of two bad ways you muft conceit me,
Either a Coward or a Flatterer.
That I did love thee *Cæfar,* O 'tis true :
If then thy Spirit look upon us now,
Shall it not grieve thee dearer then thy death,
To fee thy *Antony* making his peace,
Shaking the bloody fingers of thy Foes ?
Moft Noble, in the prefence of thy Courfe,
Had I as many eyes, as thou haft wounds,
Weeping as faft as they ftream forth thy blood,
It would become me better, then to clofe
In terms of Friendfhip with thine enemies.
Pardon me *Julius,* here waft thou bay'd brave Hart
Here did'ft thou fall, and here thy Hunters ftand
Sign'd in thy Spoil, Crimfon'd in thy Lethee.
O World ! thou waft the Forreft to this Hart,
And this indeed, O World ! the Hart of thee.
How like a Deer, ftroken by many Princes,
Doft thou here lye ?

 Caffi. Mark *Antony.*
 Ant. Pardon me *Caius Caffius* :
The Enemies of *Cæfar* fhall fay this :
Then, in a Friend, it is cold Modefty :

 Caffi. I blame you not for praifing *Cæfar* fo,
But what compact mean you to have with us ?
Will you be prick'd in number of our Friends,
Or fhall we on, and not depend on you ?

 Ant. Therefore I took your hands, but was indeed
Sway'd from the point, by looking down on *Cæfar.*
Friends am I with you all, and love you all,
Upon this hope, that you fhall give me Reafons,
Why and wherein, *Cæfar* was dangerous.

 Bru. Or elfe were this a favage Spectacle,
Our Reafons are fo full of good regard,
That were you *Antony,* the Son of *Cæfar,*
You fhall be fatisfied.   E 2

               Ant. That's

Ant. That's all I feek,
And am moreover futor, that I may
Produce his body to the Market-place,
And in the Pulpit as becomes a Friend,
Speak in the Order of his Funeral.

Bru. You fhall *Mark Antony.*

Caffi. Brutus, a wird with you:
You know not what you do, Do not confent
That *Antony* fpeak in his Funeral :
Know you how much the people may be mov'd
By that which he will utter ?

Bru. By your pardon :
I will my felf into the Pulpit firft,
And fhew the reafon of our *Cafar's* death.
What *Antony* fhall fpeak, I will proteft
He fpeaks by leave, and by permiffion :
And that we are contented *Cafar* fhall
Have all true Rites, and lawful Ceremonies,
It fhall advantage more, then do us wrong.

Caffi. I know not what may fall, I like it not.

Bru. Mark Antony, here take you *Cafar's* body ;
You fhall not in your Funeral fpeech blame us,
But fpeak all good you can devife of *Cafar,*
And fay you do't by our permiffion ;
Elfe fhall you not have any hand at all
About his Funeral, And you fhall fpeak
In the fame Pulpit where to I am going,
After my fpeech is ended.

Ant. Be it fo:
I do defire no more.

Bru. Prepare the body then, and follow us. *Exeunt.*
                        Manet Antony
O pardon me thou bleeding piece of Earth :
That I am meek and gentle with thefe Butchers.
Thou art the Ruins of the Nobleft man
That ever lived in the Tide of Times.
Woe to the hand that fhed this coftly Blood.
Over thy wounds, now do I prophefie.
(Which like dumb mouths do ope their Ruby lips,
To beg the voice and utterance of my Tongue)
A Curfe fhall light upon the limbs of men ;
Domeftick Fury, and fierce Civil ftrife,
Shall cumber all the parts of *Italy :*
Blood and deftruction fhall be fo in ufe,
And dreadful Objefts fo familiar,
That Mothers fhall but fmile; when they behold

                                        Their

Their Infants quartered with the Hands of War :
All pitty choak'd with Custom of foul deeds,
And *Cæsar*'s Spirit ranging for Revenge,
With *Ate* by his side, come hot from Hell,
Shall in these Confines with a Monarchs Voice,
Cry havock, and let slip the Dogs of War,
That this foul deed, shall smell above the Earth
With Carrion men, groaning for Burial.

Enter Octavius's *Servant*

You serve *Octavius Cæsar*, do you not ?
  Ser. I do *Mark Antony.*
  Ant Cæsar, did write for him to come to *Rome.*
  Ser. He did receive his Letters, and is coming,
And bid me say to you by word of mouth
O *Cæsar !*
  Ant. Thy heart is big : get thee a-part and weep :
Passion I see is catching from mine Eyes,
Seeing those Beads of sorrow stand in thine,
Begin to water.   Is thy Master coming ?
  Ser. He lies to night within seven Leagues of *Rome.*
  Ant. Post back with speed,
And tell him what hath chanc'd :
Here is a mourning *Rome*, a dangerous *Rome.*
No *Rome* of safety for *Octavius* yet,
Hye hence; and tell him so.   Yet stay a while,
Thou shalt not back, till I have born this course
Into the Market-place : There shall I try
In my Oration, how the People take
The cruel Issue of these bloody men ;
According to the which thou shalt discourse
To young *Octavius*, of the state of things.
Lend me your hand.   *Exeunt.*

Enter Brutus *and goes into the Pulpit, and* Cassius
with the Plebians.

  Ple. We will be satisfied : let us be satisfied.
  Bru. Then follow me, and give me Audience Friends.
Cassius go you into the other street,
And the Numbers :
Those that will hear me speak, let them stay here ;
Those that will follow *Cassius*, go with him,
And publick Reasons shall be rendred
Of *Cæsar's* death.

1. *Ple.* I will hear *Brutus* speak,
2. *I* will hear *Caffius*, and compare their Reasons,
When severally we hear them rendred.
3. The Noble *Brutus* is ascended : Silence.
Bru. Be patient till the laft.

Romans, Country-men, and Lovers. hear me for my caufe, and be filent that you may here, Believe me for mine Honour, and have refpect to mine Honour, that you may Believe, Cenfure me in your Wifdom, and awake your Senfes, that you may the better Judge : If there be any in this Affembly, any dear Friend of *Cæfar's*, to him I fay, that *Brutus* love to *Cæfar*, was no lefs then his. If then that Friend demand, why *Brutus* rofe againft *Cæfar*, this is my Anfwer : Not that I lov'd *Cæfar* lefs, but that I lov'd *Rome* more. Had you rather *Cæfar* were living, and dye all Slaves ; then that *Cæfar* were dead, to live all Free-men ? As *Cæfar* lov'd me, I weep for him ; as he was Fortunate, I rejoyce at it ; as he was Valiant, I honour him ; But as he was Ambitious, I flew him. There is Tears, for his love : Joy, for his Fortune : Honour, for his Valour : And Death for his Ambition. Who is here fo bafe, that would be a Bondman ? If any, fpeak, for him have I offended. Who is here fo rude, that would not be a *Roman ?* If any, fpeak, for him have I offended. Who is here fo vile, that will not love his Country ? If any, fpeak, for him have I offended. I paufe for a Reply.

All. None *Brutus*, none.
Bru. Then none have I offended. I have done no more to *Cæfar*, then you fhall do to *Brutus*. The Queftion of his death, is inroll'd in the Capitol ; his Glory not extenuated, wherein he was worthy ; nor his offences enforc'd, for which he fuffered death.

Enter Mark Antony, *with* Cæfar's *body.*

Here comes his Body, mourn'd by *Mark Antony*, who though he had no hand in his death, fhall receive the benefit of his dying, a Place in the Common-wealth, as which of you fhall not ? With this I depart, that as I flew my beft Lover for the good of *Rome*, I have the fame Dagger for my felf, when it fhall pleafe my Country to need my death.

All. Live *Brutus*, live, live.
1. Bring him with Triumph home unto his houfe.
2. Give him a Statue with his Anceftors.
3. Let him be *Cæfar*.
4. *Cæfar's* better parts
Shall be Crown'd in *Brutus*.
1. We'll bring him to his Houfe,
With Shouts and Clamours.
Bru. My Country-men.
2. Peace, Silence, *Brutus* fpeaks.
1. Peace ho.

                                        Bru. Good

Bru. Good Countrymen, let me depart alone,
And (for my fake) ftay here with *Antony* :
Do grace to *Cæfar's* Corps, and grace his Speech
Tending to *Cæfar's* Glories, which *Mark Antony*
(By our permiffion) is allow'd to make,
I do intreat you, not a Man depart,
Save I alone till *Antony* have fpoke.   *Exit.*

1. Stay ho, and let us hear *Mark Antony.*
3. Let him go up into the publick Chair,
We'll hear him : Noble *Antony* go up.
Ant. For *Brutus* fake, I am beholding to you.
4. What does he fay of *Brutus* ?
3. He fays for *Brutus* fake
He finds himfelf beholding to us all.
4. 'Twere beft he fpake no harm of *Brutus* here ?
1. This *Cæfar* was a Tyrant.
3. Nay that's certain :
We are bleft that *Rome* is rid of him.
2. Peace, let us hear what *Antony* can fay.
Ant. You gentle *Romans.*
All. Peace ho, let us hear him.
Ant. Friends, *Romans*, Countrymen, lend me your Ears,
I come to bury *Cæfar*, not to praife him :
The evil that men do, lives after them,
The good is oft entered with their bones,
So let it be with *Cæfar.* The Noble *Brutus,*
Hath told you *Cæfar* was Ambitious :
If it were fo it was a grievous Fault.
And grievoufly hath *Cæfar* anfwer'd it.
Here under leave of *Brutus*, and the reft
(For *Brutus* is an Honourable man,
So are they all ; all Honourable men)
Come I fpeak in *Cæfar's* Funeral.
He was my Friend, faithful and juft to me ;
But *Brutus* fays, he was Ambitious,
And *Brutus* is an Honourable man.
He hath brought many Captives home to *Rome,*
Whofe Randfoms did the general Coffers fill :
Did this in *Cæfar* feem Ambitious?
When that the Poor have cry'd, *Cæfar* hath wept :
Ambition fhould be made of fterner ftuff,
Yet *Brutus* fays he was Ambitious :
And *Brutus* is an Honourable man.
You all did fee, that on the *Lupercall,*
I thrice prefented him a Kingly Crown,
Which he did thrice refufe. Was this Ambition?

Yet *Brutus* fays he was Ambitious.
And fure he is an Honourable man.
I fpeak not to difprove what *Brutus* fpoke,
But here I am to fpeak what I do know ;
You all did love him once, not without caufe,
What caufe with-holds you then, to mourn for him?
O Judgment! thou are fled to brutifh Beafts,
And Men have loft their Reafon. Bear with me
My heart is in the Coffin there with *Cæfar*,
And I muft paufe, till it come back to me.

    1. Methinks their is much reafon in his Sayings.
    2. If thou confider rightly of the matter,
Cæfar has had great wrong.
    3. Has he Mafters? I fear there will a worfe come in his place.
    4. Mark'd yea his words? he would not take the Crown,
Therefore'tis certain, he was not Ambitious.
    1. If it be found fo, fome will near abide it.
    2. Poor foul, his Eyes are red as fire with weeping.
    3. There's not a Nobler man in *Rome* than *Antony*.
    4. Now mark him, he begins again to fpeak.
    Ant. But yefterday, the word of *Cæfar* might
Have ftood againft the World : Now lies he there ;
And none fo poor to do him reverence.
O Mafters! if I were difpofed to ftir
Your hearts and minds to Mutiny and Rage,
I fhould do *Brutus* wrong, and *Caffius* wrong :
Who (you all know) are Honourable men.
I will not do them wrong : I rather choofe
To wrong the dead, to wrong my felf and you,
Then I will wrong fuch Honourable men.
But here's a Parchment, with the Seal of *Cæfar*,
I found it in his Clofet, 'tis his Will :
Let but the Commons here his Teftament :
(Which pardon me) I do not mean to read,
And they would go and kifs dead *Cæfar*'s wounds.
And dip their Napkins in his Sacred Blood ;
Yea, beg a hair of him for Memory.
And dying, mention it within their Wills,
Bequeathing it as a rich Legacy
Unto their Iffue.
    4. We'll hear the Will, read it *Mark Antony*.
    All. The Will, the Will ; we will hear *Cæfar*'s Will.
    Ant. Have patience gentle Friends, I muft not read it.
It is not meet you know how *Cæfar* lov'd you :
You are not Wood, you are not Stones, but Men :
And being Men, hearing the Will of *Cæfar*

It will inflame you, it will make you mad ;
'Tis good you know not that you are his Heirs,
For If you fhould, O what will come of it ?

4. Read the Will, we'll hear it *Antony* :
You fhall read us the Will, *Cæfar's* Will.

Ant. Will you be patient ? Will you ftay a while ;
I have o're fhot my felf to tell you of it,
I fear I wrong the Honourable men,
Whofe Daggers have ftab'd *Cæfar* : I do fear it.

4. They were Traitors : Honourable men ?

All. The Will, the Teftament.

2. They were Villains, and Murderers : the Will, read the Will

Ant. You will compel me then to read the Will :
Then make a Ring about the Corps of *Cæfar*.
And let me fhew you him that made the Will :
Shall I defcend ? And will you give me leave ?

All. Come down.

2. Defcend.

3. You fhall have leave.

4. A Ring, ftand Round.

1. Stand from the Hearfe, ftand from the Body.

2. Room for *Antony*, moft Noble *Antony*.

Ant. Nay not fo upon me, ftand far off.

All. Stand back, room, bear back.

Ant. If you have tears, prepare to fhed them now.
You all do know this Mantle ; I remember
The firft time ever *Cæfar* put it on,
'Twas on a Summers Evening in his Tent,
That Day he overcame the *Nervii*.
Look, in the place ran *Caffius* Daggar through :
See what a rent the envious *Caska* made :
Through this, the well beloved *Brutus* ftab'd,
And as he pluck'd his curfed Steel away :
Mark how the blood of *Cæfar* follow'd it,
As rufhing out of doors, to be refolv'd
If *Brutus*, fo unkindly knock'd or no :
For *Brutus*, as you know, was *Cæfar's* Angel.
Judge, O ye Gods, how dearly *Cæfar* lov'd him,
This was the moft unkind cut of all.
For when the Noble *Cæfar* faw him ftab,
Ingratitude, more ftrong than Traitors arms,
Quite vanquifh'd him then burft his mighty heart,
And in his Mantle, Mufling up his face,
Even at the Bafe of *Pompey's* Statue
(Which all the while ran Blood) great *Cæfar* fell.
O what a fall was there, my Country-men ?

F

Then

Then I, and you, and all of us down,
Whil'ft bloody Treafon flourifh'd over us,
O now you weep, and I perceive you feel'
The dint of pitty : Thefe are gracious drops.
Kind Souls, what weep you, when you but behold
Our *Cefar*'s Vefture wounded ? Look you here,
Here is Himfelf, mar'd as you fee with Traitors.

 1 O pittyous fpectacle !
 2. O Noble *Cafar* !
 3. O woful day !
 4. O Traitors, Villains !
 1. O moft bloody fight !
 2. We will be reveng'd : Revenge
About, feek, burn, fire, kill, flay,
Let not a Traitor live.
 Ant. Stay Country-men.
 1. Peace there, hear Noble *Antony.*
 2. We'll hear him, we'll follow him, we'll die with him.
 Ant. Good Friends, fweet Friends, let me not ftir you up.
To fuch a fudden Flood of Mutiny
They that have done this Deed, are Honourable.
What private griefs they have, alas, I know not.
That made them do it : They are Wife, and Honourable,
And will no doubt with Reafons anfwer you.
I come not (Friends) to fteal away your hearts,
I am no Orator, as *Brutus* is ;
But (as you know me all) a plane blunt man :
That love my Friend, and that they know full well
That gave me publick leave to fpeak of him :
For I have neither writ, nor words, nor worth.
Action, nor Utterance, nor the power of fpeech,
To ftir mens Bloods, I only fpeak right on :
I tell you that which you your felves do know,
Shew you fweet *Cafar* wounds ; poor, poor, dumb mouths,
And bid them fpeak for me : But were I *Brutus,*
And *Brutus Antony,* there were an *Antony*
Would ruffle your Spirits, and put a Tongue
In every wound of *Cafar,* that fhould move
The ftones of *Rome,* to rife and Mutiny.
 All. We'll Mutiny.
 1. We'll burn the houfe of *Brutus.*
 3. Away then come, feek the Confpirators,
 Ant. Yet hear me Country-men yet hear me fpeak.
 All. Peace ho, hear *Antony,* moft noble *Antony.*
 Ant. Why Friends, you go to do you know not what;
Wherein hath *Cafar* thus deferv'd your loves ?

Alas

Alas you know not, I muft tell you then :
You have forgot the Will I told you of
   All. Moft true, the Will, let's ftay and here the Will!
   Ant. Here is the Will, and under *Cæfar*'s Seal.
To every *Roman* Citizen he gives,
To every feveral man, feventy five *Drachmacs.*
   2. *Ple.* Moft Noble *Cæfar*, we'll revenge his death.
   3. *Ple.* O Royal *Cæfar.*
   Ant. Hear me with Patience.
   All. Peace ho.
   Ant. Moreover he has left you all his Walks,
His private Arbors, and new-planted Orchards,
On this fide *Tyber*, he hath left them you,
And to your Heirs for ever : common Pleafures
To walk abroad and Recreate your felves.
Here was a *Cæfar :* when comes fuch another ?
   1. *Ple.* Never, never, come, away, away :
We'll burn this Body in the Holy Place,
And with the Brands fire the Traytors houfes.
Take up the Body.
   2. Go fetch fire.
   3. Pluck down Benches.
   4. Pluck down Forms, Windows any thing.   *Exeunt.*
   Ant. Now let it work : Mifchief thou art a-foot,
Take thou what courfe thou wilt.
How now Fellow ?

Enter Servant.

   Ser. Sir, *Octavius* is already come to *Rome,*
   Ant. Where is he ?
   Ser. He and *Lepidus* are at *Cæfar*'s houfe.
   Ant. And thither will I ftraight to vifit him.
He comes upon a wifh, Fortune is merry,
And in this mood will give us any thing.
   Ser. I heard him fay, *Brutus* and *Caffius*
Are rid like Madmen through the Gates of *Rome.*
   Ant. Belike they had fome notice of the People,
How I had moved them, Bring me to *Octavius. Exeunt*

Enter Cinna the Poet, and after him the Plebians.

   Cinna. I dreamt to night, that I did feaft with *Cæfar.*
And things unluckily charge my Fantafie :
I have no will to wander forth to day,
Yet fomething leads me forth.

F 2

2. What

1. What is your name?
2. Whether are you going?
3. Where do you dwell?
4. Are you a Married Man, or a Batchellor?
2. Answer every man directly.
1. I, and briefly.
4. I, and wisely.
3. I, and truly, you were beft.

Cin. What is my Name? Whither am I going? Where do I dwell? Am I a married man or a Batchellor? Then to anfwer every Man directly and briefly, wifely and truly : wifely I fay I am a Batchellor.

2. That's as much as to fay, they are Fools that marry : you'll bear me a Bang for that I fear : proceed directly.

Cinna. Directly I am going to *Cæfar*'s Funeral.

1. As a Friend, or an Enemy?

Cinna. As a Friend.

2. That matter is anfwered directly.

4. For your dwelling ; briefly.

Cinna. Briefly, I dwell by the Capitol.

3. Your Name Sir, truly.

Cinna. Truly, my Name is *Cinna.*

1. Tear him to pieces, he's a Confpirator.

Cin. I am *Cinna* the Poet, I am *Cinna* the Poet.

1. Tear him for his bad Verfes, tear him for his bad Verfes.

Cin. I am not *Cinna* the Confpirator.

4. It is no matter, his Name's *Cinna*, pluck but his Name out of his Heart, and turn him going.

3. Tear him, tear him ; Come, Brands ho, Firebrands ; to *Brutus*, to *Caffius*, burn all. Some to *Decius*'s Houfe, and fome to *Caska*'s, fome to *Ligarius*. Away go.   *Exeunt all the* Plebians.

Actus Quartus.

Enter Antony, Octavius, *and* Lepidus.

Ant. Thefe Men then fhall dye, their Names are prick'd.

Octa. Your Brother too muft dye ; confent you *Lepidus*

Lep. I do confent.

Octa. Prick him down *Antony.*

Lep. Upon Condition *Publius* fhall not live, Who is your Sifter's Son, *Mark Antony.*

              Ant. He

Ant. He shall not live ; look, with a Spot I damn him,
But *Lepidus*, go you to *Cæsar*'s house :
Fetch the Will hither, and we shall determine
How to cut off some Charge in Legacies.

Lep. What ? shall I find you here ?

Octa. Or here, or at the Capitol.

Ant. This is a slight unmeritable man,   *Exit* Lepid.
Meet to be sent on Errands : it is fit
The three-fold World divided, he should stand
One of the three to share it ?

Octa. So you though him,
And took his Voice who should be prick'd to dye
In our black Sentence and Proscription.

Ant. *Octavius*, I have seen more days than you,
And though we lay these Honours on this Man,
To ease our selves of divers sland'rous Loads,
He shall but bear them, as the Ass bears Gold,
To groan and sweat under the Business,
Either lead or driven, as we point the way :
And having brought our Treasure, where we will,
Then take we down his Load, and turn him off -
(Like to the empty Ass) to shake his Ears,
And graze in Common.

Octa. You may do your Will :
But he's a tryed, and valiant Souldier.

Ant. So is my Horse *Octavius*, and for that
I do appoint him store of Provender. -
It is a Creature that I teach to fight,
To wind, to stop run directly on :
His corporal motion, govern'd by my Spirit,
And in some tast, is *Lepidus* but so ;
He must be taught, and train'd, and bid go forth :
A barren spirited Fellow, one that feeds
On Objems, Arts and Imitations.
Which out of use, and stal'd by other Men,
Begin his Fashion. Do not take of him,
But as a Property : and now *Octavius*,
Listen great things. *Brutus* and *Cassius*
Are levying Powers : We must straight make head :
Therefore let our Alliance be combin'd,
Our best Friends made, our means stretch'd,
And let us presently go sit in Council,
How covert matters may be best disclos'd,
And open Perils surest answer'd.

Octa. Let us do so : for we are at the Stake,
And bayed about with many Enemies,

And fome that fmile have in their Hearts I fear
Millions of mifchiefs.   *Exeunt.*

Drum. Enter Brutus, Lucillius, and the Army.   Titinius
                and Pindarus *meets them.*

Bru. Stand ho.

Lucil. Give the Word ho, and ftand.

Bru. What now *Lucillius*, is *Caffius* near ?

Lucil. He is at hand, and *Pindarus* is come
To do you Salutation from his Minfter.

Bru. He greets me well.   Your Mafter *Pindarus*
In his own Charge, or by ill Officers,
Hath given me fome worthy caufe to wifh,
Things done, undone : But if he be at hand
I fhall be fatis'ied.

Pin. I do not doubt
But that my Noble Mafter will appear
Such as he is, full of Regard and Honour.

Bru. He is not doubted.   A word *Lucillius*,
How he receiv'd you : let me be refolv'd.

Lucil. With Courtefie, and with Refpect enough,
But not with fuch familiar Inftances,
Nor with fuch free and friendly Conference
As he hath us'd of old.

Bru. Thou haft defcrib'd
A hot Friend, cooling : Ever note *Lucillius*,
When Love begins to ficken and decay,
It ufeth an enforced Ceremony.
There are no tricks in plain and fimple Faith :
But hollow men, like Horfes hot at hand,
Make gallant fhew, and promife of their Mettle :
                        Low March within.
But when they fhould endure the bloody Spur,
They fall their Crefts, and like deceitful Jades,
Sink in the Trial. Come his Army on ?

Lucil. They mean this Night in *Sardis* to be quarter'd :
The great part, the Horfe in general
Are come with *Caffius*.

                Enter Caffius *and his Powers.*

Bru. Hark, he is arriv'd ;
March gently on to meet him.

Caffi. Stand ho.

Bru. Stand ho, fpeak the Word along.

Stand.

Stand.

Stand.

                                        Caffi.

Caffi. Moft Noble Brother you have done me wrong.

Bru. Judge me you Gods; wrong I mine Enemies?
And if not fo, how fhould I wrong a Brother?

Caffi. Brutus, this fober Form of yours hides Wrongs.
And when you do them————

Bru. Caffius, be content:
Speak your griefs foftly, I do know you well.
Before the eyes of both our Armies here,
(Which fhould perceive nothing but Love from us)
Let us not wrangle. Bid them move away:
Then in my Tent *Caffius* enlarge your Griefs,
And I will give you Audience.

Caffi. Pindarus,
Bid our Commanders lead their Charges off
A little from this Ground.

Bru. Lucillius, do you the like, and let no Man
Come to our Tent, till we have done our Conference.
Let *Lucius* and *Titinius* guard our door.

Manet Brutus *and* Caffius.

Exeunt.

Caffi. That you have wrong'd me, doth appear in this:
You have condemn'd, and noted *Lucius Pella*
For taking Bribes here of the *Sardians*;
Wherein my Letters, praying on his fide,
Becaufe I knew the Man was flighted off.

Bru. You wrong'd your felf to write in fuch a Cafe.

Caffi. In fuch a time as this, it is not meet
That every nice Offence fhould bear his Comment.

Bru. Let me tell you *Caffius,* you your felf
Are much condemn'd to have an itching Palm,
To fell, and mart your Offices for Gold,
To Undefervers.

Caffi. I an itching Palm?
You know that you are *Brutus* that fpeaks this,
Or by the Gods, this Speech were elfe your laft.

Bru. The Name of *Caffius* honours this Corruption,
And Chaftifement doth therefore hide his Head.

Caffi. Chaftifement?

Bru. Remember *March,* the Ides of *March* remember:
Did not great *Julius* bleed for Juftice fake?
What Villain touch'd his Body, that did ftab,
And not for Juftice? What? Shall one of Us,
That ftruck the fore-moft man of all this World,
But for fupporting Robbers; fhall we now,
Contaminate our Fingers with bafe Bribes?
And fell the mighty fpace of our large Honours,
For fo much Trafh as may be grafped thus?

J

I had rather be a Dog, and bay the Moon,
Than fuch a *Roman*.

Caſſi. *Brutus* ; bait not me,
I'll not endure it : you forget your ſelf
To hedge me in. I am a Souldier, I,
Older in Practice, abler than your ſelf
To make Conditions.

Bru. Go too, you are not *Caſſius.*

Caſſi. I am.

Bru. I ſay you are not.

Caſſi. Urge me no more, I ſhall forget my ſelf ;
Have mind upon your Health : Tempt me no farther.

Bru. Away ſlight man.

Caſſi. Is't poſſible ;

Bru. Hear me, for I will ſpeak.
Muſt I give way and room to your raſh Choler ?
Shall I be frighted when a Mad-man ſtares ?

Caſſi. O ye Gods, ye Gods, Muſt I endure all this ?

Bru. All this ? I more : Fret till your proud Heart break.
Go ſhew your Slaves how cholerick you are,
And make your Bondmen tremble, muſt I bow ?
Muſt I obſerve you ? Muſt I ſtand and crouch
Under your teſty Humour ? By the Gods,
You ſhall digeſt the Venom of your Spleen,
Though it do ſplit you. For, from this day forth,
I'll uſe you for my Mirth, ye for my Laughter,
When you are Waſpiſh.

Caſſi. Is it come to this ?

Bru. You ſay, you are a better Souldier :
Let it appear ſo ; make your vaunting true,
And it ſhall pleaſe me well, For my own part,
I ſhall be glad to learn of Noble-men,

Caſſi. You wrong me every way :
You wrong me *Brutus* :
I ſaid, an Elder Souldier, not a Better
Did I ſay Better ?

Bru. If you did, I care not.

Caſſi. When *Cæſar* liv'd, he durſt not thus have mov'd me.

Bru. Peace, Peace, you durſt not ſo have tempted him.

Caſſi. I durſt not ?

Bru. No.

Caſſi. What ! durſt not tempt him ?

Bru. For your Life you durſt not.

Caſſi. Do not preſume too much upon my Love,
I may do that I ſhall be ſorry for

Bru. You

Bru. You have done that you should be sorry for.
There is no Terror *Cassius* in your Threats:
For I am arm'd so strong in Honesty.
That they pass by me, as the idle Wind,
Which I respect not, I did send to you
For certain Sums of Gold, which you deny'd me.
For I can raise no Money by vile means:
By Heavens, I had rather Coin my Heart,
And drop my Blood for Drachmaes, than to wring
From the hard hands of Peasants, their vile Trash
By any Indirection. I did send
To you for Gold to pay my Legions,
Which you deny'd me: was that done like *Cassius?*
Should I have answer'd *Caius Cassius* so?
When *Marcus Brutus* grows so Covetous,
To lock such Rascal Counters from his Friends,
Be ready Gods, with all your Thunder-bolts,
Dash him to pieces.

Cassi. I deny'd you not.

Bru. You did.

Cassi. I did not, He was but a Fool
That brought my Answer back. *Brutus* hath riv'd my heart.
A Friend should bear his Infirmities;
But *Brutus* makes mine greater than they are.

Bru. I do not, till you practice them on me.

Cassi. You love me not.

Bru. I do not like your Faults.

Cassi. A Friendly Eye could never see such Faults.

Bru. A Flatterers would not, though they do appear
As huge as high *Olympus.*

Cassi. Come *Antony,* and young *Octavius* come,
Revenge your selves alone on *Cassius,*
For *Cassius* is a-weary of the World:
Hated by one he loves, brav'd by his Brother,
Cheek'd like a bond-man, all his Faults observ'd,
Set in a Note Book, learn'd, and con'd by roat
To cast into my Teeth. O I could weep
My Spirits from my Eyes. There is my Dagger,
And here my naked Breast; Within, a Heart
Dearer than *Pluto*'s Mine, richer than Gold,
If that thou beest a *Roman,* take it forth.
I that deny'd thee Gold, will give my Heart;
Strike as thou didst at *Cæsar*; For I know,
When thou didst hate him worse, thou loved'st him better
Than ever thou lovest *Cassius.*

G

Bru.

Bru. Sheath your Dagger :
Be angry when you will, it fhall have Scope :
Do what you will, Difhonour fhall be Humour.
O *Caffius,* you are voaked with a Lamb
That carries Anger, as the Flint bears Fire,
Who much inforced, fhews a hafty Spark,
And ftrait is cold again.

Caffi. Hath *Caffius* liv'd
To be but Mirth and Laughter to his *Brutus,*
When Grief and Blood ill temper'd vexeth him ?

Bru. When I fpoke that, I was ill temper'd too :

Caffi. Do you confefs fo much ? give me your Hand.

Bru. And my Heart too.

Caffi. O *Brutus.*

Bru. What's the matter ?

Caffi. Have not you Love enough to bear with me,
When that rafh Humour which my Mother gave me
Makes me forgetful ?

Bru. Yes *Caffius,* and from henceforth,
When you are over-earneft with your *Brutus,*
He'll think your Mother chides, and leave you fo.

Enter a Poet.

Poet. Let me go in to fee the Generals ;
There is fome Grudg between 'em, 'tis not meet
They be alone.

Lucil. You fhall not come to them.

Poet. Nothing but Death fhall ftay me.

Caffi. How now ? what's the matter ?

Poet. For fhame you Generals ; what do you mean ?
Love and be Friends, as two fuch Men fhould be,
For I have feen more years I'm fure than ye.

Caffi. Ha, ha, how vilely doth this *Cynick* Rhyme ?

Bru. Get you hence Sirrah. Saucy Fellow, hence.

Caffi. Bear with him *Brutus,* 'tis his Fafhion ;

Bru. I'll know his humour, when he knows his time :
What fhould the Wars do with thefe Jigging Fools ?
Companion, hence.

Caffi. Away, away, be gone.   *Exit* Poet.

Bru. *Lucillius* and *Titinius,* bid the Commanders
Prepare to lodge their Companies to night.

Caffi. And come your felves, and bring *Meffala* with you
Immediately to us.

Bru. *Lucius,* a Bowl of Wine.

                                        Caffi.

Caff. I did not think you could have been so angry.

Bru. O *Caffius,* I am sick of many Griefs.

Caff. Of your **Philofophy you make no ufe,**
If you give place to accidental Evils.

Bru. No man bears Sorrow better, *Portia* is dead.

Caff. Ha! *Portia?*

Bru. She is dead.

Caff. How scap'd I killing, when I croft you so?
O infupportable and touching lofs!
Upon what Sicknefs?

Bru. Impatient of my abfence.
And grief, that young *Octavius* with *Mark Antony,*
Have made themfelves so ftrong: For with her death
That Tidings came. With this fhe fell diftracted,
And (her Attendants abfent) fwallow'd fire.

Caff. And dy'd so?

Bru. Even so.

Caff. O ye immortal Gods!

Enter Boy with Wine and Tapers.

Bru. Speak no more of her; Give me a Bowl of Wine,
In this I bury all Unkinpnefs *Caffius.*   *Drinks.*

Caff. My heart is thirfty for that noble pledge.
Fill *Lucius,* till the Wine o're-fwell the Cup?
I cannot drink too much of *Brutus* Love.

Enter Titinius and Meffella.

Bru Come in *Titinius*;
Welcome good *Meffella*;
Now fit we clofe about this Taper here,
And call in queftion our Neceffities.

Caff. *Portia,* art thou gone?

Bru. No more I pray you.
Meffella, I have here received Letters,
That young *Octavius,* and *Mark Antony,*
Come down upon us with a mighty Power,
Bending there Expedition toward *Philippi*

Meff. My felf have Letters of the felf fame Tenure.

Bru. With what Addition?

Meff. That by Profcription, and bills of Outlary
Octavius, Antony, and *Lepidus.*
Have put to Death an hundred Senators.

Bru. Therein our Letters do not well agree:
Mine fpeak of feventy Senators that dy'd
By there Procriptions, *Cicero* being one.

Caff.

Caſſi. *Cicero* one ?

Meſſa. *Cicero* is dead, and by that order of Proſcription
Had you your Letters from your Wife, my Lord ?

Bru. No *Meſſala.*

Meſſa. Nor nothing in your Letters writ of her ?

Bru. Nothing *Meſſala.*

Meſſa. That methinks is ſtrange.

Bru. Why ask you ?
Hear you ought of her in yours ?

Meſſa. No my Lord.

Bru. Now as you are a *Roman* tell me true.

Meſſa. Then like a *Roman.* bear the Truth I tell.
For certain ſhe is dead, and by ſtrange manner.

Bru. Why Farewel *Portia* We muſt dye *Meſſala* :
With meditating that ſhe muſt dye once.
I have the Patience to endure it now.

Meſſa. Even ſo great Men great Loſſes ſhould endure.

Caſſi. I have as much of this in Art as you,
But yet my Nature could not bear it ſo.

Bru. Well, to your Work alive. What do you think
Of marching to *Philippi* preſently.

Caſſi. I do not think it good.

Bru. Your reaſon ?

Caſſi. This it is :
'Tis better that the Enemy ſeek us,
So ſhall he waſte his Means weary his Souldiers,
Doing himſelf offence, whilſt we lying ſtill
Are full to Reſt, Defence, and Nimbleneſs.

Bru. Good Reaſons muſt of force give place to better :
The Poeple 'twixt *Philippi* and this Ground,
Do ſtand but in a forc'd affection :
For they have grudg'd us Contribution.
The Enemy, marching along by them,
By them ſhall make a fuller number up,
Come on refreſhed, new added, and encourag'd ;
From which advantage ſhall we cut him off ;
If at *Philippi* we do face him their,
Theſe People at our back.

Caſſi. Hear me good Brother.

Bru. Under your pardon. You muſt note beſide,
That we have try'd the utmoſt of our Friends :
Our Legions are brim full, our Cauſe is ripe,
The Enemy encreaſeth every day,
We at the height, are ready to decline.
There is a Tide in the Affairs of Men
Which taken at the Flood, leads on to Fortune ;

Omitted,

Omitted, all the Voyage of their Life
Is bound in Shallows, and in Miferies.
On fuch a full Sea are we now a-float,
And we muft take the Current when it ferves,
Or lofe our Ventures.

Caſſi. Then with your Will, go on? we'll along
Our felves, and meet them at *Philippi.*

Bru. The deep of Night is crept upon our Talk,
And Nature muft obey Neceſſity
Which we will niggard with a little Reſt:
There is no more to fay.

Caſſi. No more, good night,
Early to morrow will we rife, and hence.

Enter Lucius.

Bru. Lucius, my Gown Farewel good *Meſſala,*
Good night *Titinius*; Noble *Caſſius,*
Good night, and good repofe.

Caſſi. O my dear Brother;
This was an ill beginning of the Night;
Never come fuch Divifion 'tween our Souls:
Let it not *Brutus.*

Enter Lucius *with the Gown.*

Bru. Every thing is well.
Caſſi. Good night my Lord.
Bru. Good night good Brother.
Tit. Meſſala. Good night Lord *Brutus.*
Bru. Farewel every one.
Give me the Gown.   Where is thy Inftrument?   *Exeunt.*
Luc. Here in the Tent.
Bru. What, thou fpeak'ft drowfily;
Poor Knave, I blame thee not, thou art o're-watch'd,
Call *Claudio,* and fome other of my Men,
I'll have them fleep on Coufhions in my Tent.
Luc. Varrus, and *Claudio?*

Enter Varrus *and* Claudio.

Var. Calls my Lord?
Bru. I pray you Sirs, lye in my Tent and fleep.
It may be I fhall raife you by and by
On bufinefs to my Brother *Caſſius.*

                                                        Var. So

Var. So pleafe you, we will ftand,
And watch your Pleafure.

Bru. I will not have it fo: Lye down good Sirs,
It may be I fhall otherwife bethink me.
Look *Lucius,* here's the Book I fought for fo:
I put it in the Pocket of my Gown.

Luc. I was fure your Lordfhip did not give it me.

Bru. Bear with me, good Boy, I am much forgetful.
Can'ft thou hold up thy heavy eyes a while,
And touch thy Inftrument a Strain or two.

Luc. I my Lord, can't pleafe you.

Bru. It does, my Boy:
I trouble thee too much, but thou art willing.

Luc. It is my Duty, Sir.

Bru. I fhould not urge thy Duty paft thy Might,
I know young Bloods look for a time of reft.

Luc. I have flept my Lord already.

Bru. It was well done, and thou fhalt fleep again:
I will not hold thee long. If I do live,
I will be good to thee.

Mufick and a Song.

This is a fleepy Tune: O murd'rous Slumber!
Layeft thou thy leaden Mace upon my Boy,
That plays the Mufick? Gentle Knave good night:
I will not do thee foo much wronft to wake thee:
If thou do'ft nod, thou break'ft thy Inftrument,
I'll take it from thee, and (good Boy) good night:
Let me fee, let me fee; is not the Leaf turn'd down
Where I left reading? Here it is, I think.

Enter the Ghoft of Cæfar.

How ill this Toper burns. Ha! Who comes here?
I think it is the weaknefs in mine Eyes
That fhapes this monftrous Apparition.
It comes upon me: Art thou any thing;
Art thou fome God, fome Angel, or fome Devil,
That makeft my Blood cold, and my Hair to ftare?
Speak to me, what thou art.

Ghoft. Thy evil Spirit *Brutus.*

Bru. Why com'ft thou?

Ghoft. To tell thee thou fhalt fee me at *Philippi.*

Bru. Well: then I fhall fee thee again?

Ghoft. I, at *Philippi.*

Bru. Why I will fee thee at *Philippi* then:
Now I have taken Heart thou vanifheft.

I'll

I'll Spirit, I would hold more talk with thee.
Boy, *Lucius*, *Claudio*, Sirs, Awake:
Claudio.

Luc. The Strings, my Lord, are falfe.

Bru. He thinks he ftill is at his Inftrument ;
Lucius, awak.

Luc. My Lord.

Bru. Did'ft thou dream, *Lucius*, that thou fo cryed'ft out.

Luc. My Lord, I do not know that I did cry.

Bru. Yes that thou didft ; Didft thou fee any thing ?

Luc. Nothing, my Lord.

Bru. Sleep again *Lucius* : Sirrah, *Claudio*, Fellow,
Thou : Awake.

Var. My Lord.

Clau. My Lord.

Bru. Why did you fo cry out Sirs, in your Sleep ?

Both. Did we, my Lord ?

Bru. I, faw you any thing ?

Var. No, my Lord, I faw nothing.

Clau. Nor I my Lord.

Bru. Go, and commend me to my Brother *Caffius* :
Bid him put on his Powers betimes before,
And we will follow.

Both. It fhall be done, my Lord.   *Exeunt.*

Actus Quintus.

Enter, Octavius, Antony, and their Army.

Octa. Now *Antony*, our hopes are anfwered,
You faid the Enemy would not come down,
But keep the Hills and upper Regions :
It proves not fo : their Battles are at hand,
They mean to warm us at *Philippi* here :
Anfwering before we do demand of them.

Ant. But, I am in their Bofoms, and I know
Wherefore they do it : They could be content
To vifit other places, and come down
With fearful Bravery : thinking by this Face
To faften in our Thoughts that they have Courage ;
But 'tis not fo.

Enter a Meffenger.

Meff. Prepare you Generals,
The Enemy comes on in gallant fhew.

There

Their bloody Sign of Battle is hung out,
And fomething to be done imediately.
Ant. *Octavius,* lead your Battle foftly on
Upon the left hand of the even Field.
Octa. Upon the right hand I, keep you the left.
Ant. Why do you crofs me in this Exigent?
Octa. I do not crofs you, but I will do fo.   *March.*

    Drum.   *Enter* Brutus, Caffius *and their Army.*

Bru. They ftand, and would have Parly.
Caffi. Stand faft *Titinius,* we muft out and talk:
Octa. *Mark Antony,* fhall we give fign of Battle?
Ant. No *Cæfar,* we will anfwer on their Charge.
Make forth the Generals would have fome Words.
Octa. Stir not until the Signal.
Bru. Words before blows; is it fo Countrymen?
Octa. Nor that we love Words better, as you do.
Bru. Good Words is better than bad Strokes, *Octavius*
   Ant. In your bad Strokes, *Brutus,* you give good Words.
Witnefs the hole you made in *Cæfar's* heart,
Crying, long live, Hail *Cæfar.*
  Caffi. Antony.
The pofture of your blows are yet unknown;
But for your words, they rob the *Hibla* Bees,
And leave them Honnylefs.
   Ant. Not Stinglefs too.
   Bru. O yes, and Squndlefs too.
For you have ftolen their Buzzing, *Antony*
And very wifely Threat before you Sting.
   Ant. Villains, you did not fo, when your vile daggers
Hackt one another in the Sides of *Cæfar;*
You fhew'd your Teeth like Apes,
And fawn'd like Hounds,
And bow'd like Bondmen, kiffing *Cæfar's* feet;
Whilft damned *Caska,* like a Cur, behind
Strook *Cæfar* on the Neck. O you Flatterers!
   Caffi. Flatterers? Now *Brutus* thank your felf;
This Tongue had not offered fo to Day,
If *Caffius* might have Rul'd.
   Octa. Come, come, the Caufe; if Arguing makes us Swear,
The proof of it will turn to redder drops:
Look I draw a Sword againft Confpirators;
When think you that the Sword goes up again?
Never till *Cæfar's* Three and Thirty wounds
Be well avenged; or till another *Cæfar*

                           Have

Have added flaughter to the Sword of Traitors

Bru. *Cæsar*, thou canft not dye by Traitors hands,
Unlefs thou bring'ft them with thee.

Octa. So I hope.
I was not born to dye on *Brutus* Sword.

Bru. O If thou war't the Nobleft of the Strain.
Young-man, thou could'ft not dye more honourable,

Caffi. A peevifh School-boy, worthlefs of fuch Honour.
Joyn'd with a Masker, and a Reveller,

Ant. Old *Caffius* ftill.

Octa. Come *Antony*, away :
Defiance Traytors, hurl we in your teeth.
If you dare fight to day, come to the Field,
If not when you have ftomacks.

Exit Octavius, Antony, *and Army.*

Caffi. Why now blow wind, fwell Billow,
And fwim Bark :
The ftorm is up, and all is on the hazard.

Bru. Ho *Lucillius*, hark, a word with you.

Lucillius *and* Meffala *ftand forth.*

Luc. My Lord.

Caffi. *Meffala.*

Meffa. What fays my General ?

Caffi. *Meffala*, this is my Birth day, as this very day
Was *Caffius* Born.   Give me thy hand *Meffala.*
Be thou my witnefs that againft my will
(As *Pompey* was) am I compel'd to fet
Upon one Battle all our Liberties,
You know, that I held *Epicurus* ftrong,
And his Opinion : Now I change my mind,
And partly credit things that do prefage.
Coming from *Sardis* on our former Enfign
Two mighty Eagles fell, and there they pearch'd ;
Gorging and feeding from our Souldiers hands,
Who to *Philippi* here conforted us :
This Morning are they fled away, and gone,
And in their fteads, do Ravens, Crows, and Kites
Fly o're our heads, and downward look on us :
As we where fickly prey ; their fhadows feem
A Canopy moft fatal, under which
Our Army lies, ready to give up the Ghoft.

Meffa. Believe not fo.

Caffi. I but belive it partly,
For I am frefh of fpirit, and refolv'd
To meet all perils, very Conftantly.

Bru. Even fo *Lucillius.*

H.

Caffi

Caſſi. Now moſt Noble, *Brutus,*
The Gods to day ſtand friendly, that we may
Lovers in peace, lead on our days to Age.
But ſince the affairs of men reſt ſtill incert
Let's reaſon with the worſt that may befal.
If we do loſe this Battail, than is this
The very laſt time we ſhall ſpeake together :
What are you then determined to do ?
  Bru. Even by the rule of that Philoſophy,
By which I did blame *Cato,* for the death
Which he did give himſelf, I know not how :
But I do find it Cowardly, and vile
For fear of what might fall, ſo to prevent
The time of Life, arming my ſelf with patience,
To ſtay the providence of ſome high Powers,
That govern us below.
  Caſſi. Then, if we loſe this Battail,
You are contented to be led in Triumph
Thorow the Streets of *Rome.*
  Bru. No *Caſſius,* no :
Think not, thou Noble *Roman,*
That ever *Brutus* will go bound to *Rome,*
He bears too great a mind, But this ſame day
Muſt end that work, the *Ides* of *March* begun
And whether we ſhall meet again, I know not :
Therefore our everlaſting farewel take :
For ever, and for ever, farewel *Caſſius,*
If we do meet again, why we ſhall ſmile :
If not, why then this parting was well made,
  Caſſi. For ever, and for ever, farewel *Brutus*
If we do meet again, we'll ſmile indeed ;
If not 'tis true, this parting was well made.
  Bru. Why then lead on, O that a man might know
The end of this days buſineſs, e're it come :
But it ſufficeth, that the day will end.
And then the end is known, Come ho, away.   *Exeunt.*

      Alarums.   *Enter* Brutus *and* Meſſala.

  Bru. Ride, ride *Meſſala,* ride and give theſe bills
Unto the Legions, on the other ſide.
                           Lowd Alarum.

Let them ſet on at once, for I perceive
But cold demeanor in *Octavio's* wing :
And ſudden puſh gives them the overthrow :   *Exeunt.*
Ride, ride *Meſſala,* let them all come down.
                           Alarum.

Alarums.   *Enter* Cassius *and* Titinius

Cass. O look *Titinius*, look the Villains fly :
My felf have to mind own turn'd Enemy ;
This Enfign here of mine was turning back,
I flew the Coward, and did take it from him.

Tit. O *Caffius, Brutus* gave the word too early,
Who having fome advantage on *Octavius*,
Took it too eagarly ; his Souldiers fell to fpoil,
Whil'ft we by *Antony* are all inclos'd,

Enter Pindarus.

Pind. Fly further off, my Lord, fly further off,
Mark Antony is in your Tents, my Lord ;
Fly therefore Noble *Caffius*, fly far off.

Caffi. This Hill is far enough. Look, look *Titinius*,
Are not thofe my Tents whare I perceive the Fire ?

Tit. They are, my Lord.

Caffi. *Titinius*, If thou loveft me,
Mount thou my horfe, and hide thy Spurs in him,
Till he have brought thee up to yonder Troops,
And here again, that I may reft affur'd
Whether yond Troops are Friend or Enemy.

Tit. I will be here again, even with a thought.   *Ex.*

Caffi. Go *Pindarus*, get higher on that hill,
My fight was ever thick : regard *Titinius*,
And tell me what thou not'ft about the Field.
This day I breathed firft, time is come round,
And where I did begin, their fhall I end,
My life is run his compafs. Sirrah, what news ?

Pin. Above, O my Lord.

Caffi. What news ?

Pin. *Titinius* is inclofed round about.
With horfmen, that make to him on the Spur,
Yet he fpurs on, Now they are almoft on him.
Now *Titinius*, now fome light : O ! now he lights too,
He's tane.   *Shout.*
And hark, they fhout for joy.

Caffi. Come down, behold no more :
O Coward that I am, to live fo long,
To fee my Friend tane before my face.

Enter Pindarus.

Come hither firrah ; in *Parthia* did I take thee Prifoner,
And then I fwore thee, faving of thy Life,

That

That whatfoever I did bid thee do,
Thou fhouldft attempt it, Come now keep thine Oath,
Now be a Free-man, and with this good Sword
That ran through *Cæfar*'s bowels, fearch this bofom.
Stand not to anfwer : Here take thou the Hilts,
And when my face is cover'd, as 'tis now,
Guide thou the Sword——*Cæfar*, thou art reveng'd
Even with the Sword that kill'd thee.

Pin. So, I am free,
Yet would not fo have been
Durft I have done my will, O *Caffius!*
Far from this Country *Pindarus* fhall run,
Where never *Roman* fhall take note of him.

Enter Titinius *and* Meffala.

Meffa. It is but change, *Titinius*; for *Octavius*
Is overthrown by Noble *Brutus* power,
As *Caffius* Legions are by *Antony*.

Titin. Thefe tydings will well comfort *Caffius*.

Meffa. Where did you leave him?

Titin. All difconfolate.
With *Pindarus* his Bondman, on this Hill.

Meffa. Is not that he that lyes upon the ground?

Titin. He lies not like the Living, O my heart?

Meffa. Is not that he?

Titin. No, this was he *Meffala*,
But *Caffius* is no more. O fetting Sun;
As in thy red Rays thou do'ft fink to night;
So in his red blood *Caffius* day is fet.
The Sun of *Rome* is fet, Our day is gone,
Clowds, Dews, and Dangers come; our deeds are done;
Miftruft of my fuccefs hath done this deed.

Meffa. Miftruft of good fuccefs hath done this deed;
O hateful Error, Melancholies Child :
Why do'ft thou fhew to the apt thoughts of men
The things that are not? O Error foon conceiv'd,
Thou never com'ft unto a happy birth,
But kill'ft the Mother that engendred thee.

Titin. What *Pindarus?* Where art thou *Pindarus?*

Meffa. Seek him *Titinius*, whilft I go to meet
The Noble *Brutus*, thrufting this report
Into his ears; I may fay thrufting it:
For piercing Steell, and Darts invenomed,
Shall be as welcome to the ears of *Brutus*,
As tydings of this fight.

Titin.

Titin. Hye you *Meſſala,*
And I will ſeek for *Pindarus* the while :
Why didſt thou ſend me forth brave *Caſſius* ?
Did I not meet thy Friends, and did not they
Put on my Brows this wrath of Victory,
And bid me give it thee ? Did'ſt thou not hear their ſhowts ?
Alas, thou haſt miſconſtrued every thing.
But hold thee, take this Garland on thy Brow,
Thy *Brutus* bid me give it thee, and I
Will do his bidding. *Brutus,* come apace,
And ſee how I regarded *Caius Caſſius* :
By your leave Gods ; This is a *Roman* part,
Come *Caſſius* Swofd, and find *Titinius* heart.   *Dies.*

    Alarum.   *Enter* Brutus, Meſſala, *young* Cato,
        Srato, Volumoius, *and* Lucillius.

Bru. Where, where *Meſſala* doth his body lye ?
Meſſa. Loe yonder, and *Titinius* mourning it.
Bru. *Titinius* face is upwards.
Cato. He is ſlain.
Bru. O *Julius Cæſar,* thou art mighty yet,
Thy Spirit walks abroad, and turns our Swords
In our own proper Entrails.   *Low Alarums.*
    Cato. Brave *Titinius.*
Look where he have not Crown'd dead *Caſſius.*
    Bru. Are yet two *Romans* living ſuch as theſe ;
The laſt of all the *Romans,* far thee well :
It is impoſſible, that ever *Rome*
Should breed thy fellow, Friends I own my tears
To this dead man, than you ſhall ſee me pay.
I ſhall find time, *Caſſius* I ſhall find time,
Come therefore, and *Tharſus* ſend his body,
His Funerls ſhall not be in our Camp,
Left it diſcomfort us, *Lucillius* come,
And come young *Cato,* let us to the Field,
Labio and *Flavio* ſet our Battails on,
'Tis three a Clock, and *Romans* yet e're night,
We ſhall try Fortune in a ſecond Fight.   *Exeunt.*

    Alarum.   *Enter* Brutus, Meſſala, Cato, Lucillius,
        and Flavius.

Bru. Yet Country-men : O yet hold up your heads.
   Cato. What Baſtard doth not ? Who will go with me.
I will proclaim my name about the Field.

                              I am

I am the Son of *Marcus Cato*, ho.
A Foe of Tyrants, and my Countries Friend.
I am the Son of *Marcus Cato*, ho.   *Exeunt.*

Enter Soldiers, and fight.

Bru. And I am *Brutus*. *Marcus Brutus* I,
Brutus my Countries Friend : Know me for *Brutus.*
  Luc. O young and Noble *Cato*, art thou down ?
Why now thou dyeſt as bravely as *Titinius,*
And may'ſt be honour'd being *Cato's* Son.
  Sold. Yield, or thou dieſt.
  Luc. Only I yield to die :
There is ſo much, that thou wilt kill me ſtraight :
Kill *Brutus,* and he honour'd in his death.
  Sold. We muſt not : A Noble Priſoner.

Enter Antony.

  2. *Sold.* Room ho : tell *Antony, Brutus* is tane.
  1. *Sold.* I'll tell the news.   Here comes the General,
Brutus is tane, *Brutus* is tane, my Lord.
  Ant. Where is he ?
  Luc. Safe *Antony, Brutus* it ſafe enough :
I dare aſſure thee, that no Enemy
Shall ever take alive the Noble *Brutus*
The Gods defend him from ſo great a ſhame.
When you do find him, or alive, or dead ;
He will be found like *Brutus,* like himſelf.
  Ant. This is not *Brutus* friend, but I aſſure you,
A prize no leſs in worth ; keep this man ſafe,
Give him all kindneſs, I had rather have
Such men my Friends than Enemies.   Go on,
And ſee where *Brutus* be alive or dead,
And bring us word, unto *Octavius* Tent :
How every thing is chang'd.

Enter Brutus, Dardanius, Clitus, Streto,
and Volumnius.

  Bru. Come poor remains of friends, reſt on this Rock.
  Clit. Statillius, ſhew'd the Torch-light, but my Lord,
He came not back ; he is tane, or ſlain.
  Bru. Sit thee down, *Clitus :* ſlaying is the word,
It is a deed in faſhion.   Hark thee, *Clitus,*
  Clit. What I, my Lord ? No, not for all the World.

                                                    Bru.

Bru. Peace then, no words.

Clit. I'le rather kill my self.

Bru. Hark thee, *Dardanius.*

Dard. Shall I do such a deed?

Clit. O *Dardanius.*

Dard. O *Clitus.*

Clit. What ill request did *Brutus* make to thee?

Dard. To kill him, *Clitus:* look he mediates.

Clit. Now is that Noble Vessel full of grief,
That it runs over even at his eyes.

Bru. Come hither, good *Volumnius,* list a word.

Volum. What says my Lord?

Bru. Why this, *Volumnius:*
The Ghost of *Cæsar* hath appear'd to me
Two several times by Night: at *Sardis,* once;
And this last Night, here in *Philippi* Fields:
I know my hour is come.

Volum. Not so my Lord.

Bru. Nay, I am sure it is, *Volumnius.*
Thou see'st the World, *Volumnius,* how it goes,   *Low Alarum.*
Our Enemies have beat us to the Pit:
It is more worthy, to leap in our selves,
Then tarry till they push us. Good *Volumnius,*
Thou know'st, that we two went to School together.
Even for that our love of old, I prethee
Hold thou my Swords Hilt, whilst I run on it.

Volum. That's not an Office for a friend, my Lord.
     Alarum still.

Clit. Fly, fly my Lord, there is no tarrying here.

Bru. Farewel to you, and you *Volumnius.*
Strato, thou hast been all this while a sleep:
Farewel to thee, to *Strato,* Countrymen:
My heart doth joy, that yet in all my life,
I found no man, but he was true to me.
I shall have glory by this losing day
More then *Octavius,* and *Mark Antony,*
By this vile Conquest shall attain unto.
So fare you well at once, for *Brutus* tongue
Hath almost ended his lives History:
Night hangs upon mine eyes, my Bnoes wou'd rest,
That have but labour'd, to attain this hour.
     Alarum.   *Cry within, Fly, fly, fly.*

Clit. Fly my Lord, fly.

Bru. Hence: I will follow:
I prethee *Strato,* stay thou by thy Lord,
Thou art a Fellow of a good respect:

thy

Thy life hath had fome fmatch of Honour in it,
Hold then my Sword, and turn away thy face,
While I do run upon it, Wilt thou *Strato*.

  Stra. Give me thy hand firft, Fare you well my Lord.

  Bru. Farewel good *Strato*——*Cæfar*, now be ftill,
I Kil!'d not thee with half fo good a will.   *Dyes.*

      Alarum. Retreat, Enter Antony, Octavius, Meffala.
         Lucillius, *and the Army.*

  Octa. What man is that?

  Meffa. My Mafters man, *Strato*, where is thy Mafter?

  Stra. Free from the Bondage you are in *Meffala*,
The Conquerors can but make a fire of him:
For *Brutus* only overcame himfelf,
And no man elfe hath Honour by his death.

  Lucil. So *Brutus* fhould be found, I thank the *Brutus*
That thou haft prov'd *Lucillius* faying true.

  Octa. All that ferv'd *Brutus*, I will entertain them,
Fellow, wilt thou beftow thy time with me?

  Stra. I if *Meffala* will prefer me to you.

  Octa. Do fo, good *Meffala.*

  Meffa. How dyed my Mafter *Strato?*

  Stra. I held the Sword, and he did run on it,

  Meffa. Octavius then take him to follow thee,
That did the lateft fervice to my Mafter.

  Ant. This was the Nobleft *Roman* of them all:
All the Confpirators, fave only he,
Did that they did in envy of great *Cæfar*:
He, only in a general honeft thought,
And common good to all, made one of them.
His life was gentle, and the Elements
So mixt in him, that Nature might ftand up,
And fay to all the World; This was a man.

  Octa. According to his Vertue, let us ufe him
With all Refpect, and Rites of Burial.
Within my Tent his bones to night fhall lye,
Moft like a Souldier ordered Honourably:
So call the Field to reft, and let's away,
To part the glories of this happy day.   *Exeunt omnes.*

F I N I S.